STREET FOOD ASIA

LUKE NGUYEN

PHOTOGRAPHY BY ALAN BENSON

hardie grant books

Whether eating fiery som tum on a bustling Bangkok street, slurping phở in Vietnam perched on a red plastic stool, inhaling the galangal, lemongrass and coconut-infused air of Jakarta, or being seduced by heady wafts of succulent satay as it grills in Kuala Lumpur, there's nothing more alluring than street food. I love, love, love it, in all its permutations. When I travel, my top priority is hitting the pavement in search of interesting things to eat, making sure I do this at a slow pace and with my ears, eyes and nose on constant red alert. Down alleys and around every bend in the road, there's a tucked-away kitchen or mobile cart dispensing hot, smoky, freshly cooked deliciousness and I don't want to miss a single edible thing.

Discovering local street food is the best way I know to understand a place and instantly feel connected to it. It's my ultimate buzz and the fact that it comes complete with flames, steam, smoke, smells, sounds, colour, heat, energy, good vibes and a ton of flavour, only makes it better. Now I want to take you with me on an adventure to some of my favourite Asian nooks and crannies – places where fantastic street food still reigns supreme.

All over South-East Asia, the street food repertoire is vast. Getting to know every dish and its regional spin-offs would take a lifetime and that's part of the allure – there's so much to know and I'm constantly making new discoveries. The adventure isn't just about uncovering the technicalities of a particular dish though as there are also, invariably, fascinating backstories and compelling snippets of family and food history involved. And then there are the dedicated cooks. I love watching street cooks work; I love hearing their stories, I love seeing the skill, care and passion they put into every dish they make. Cooks tend to be generous people and nowhere more so than on the street – I gain so much in knowledge and in my humanity every time I get out among authentic street food action.

According to the Food and Agriculture Organization of the United Nations, 2.5 billion people globally eat street food every day. Street food evolved around necessity; people had tiny living spaces so home kitchens weren't an option and, in some countries, this still holds true for many. Mobile food hawking is a way to get nutritious, affordable, varied, ready-cooked food to the urban masses while supporting local economies; food vendors tend to purchase from the nearest market, stocked with local produce, according to what is in season. Less tangible benefits of street food culture include the preservation of traditional cooking styles and the fostering of community. Yes, street cooking is evolving, particularly in more developed places. But most often, street food dishes are cooked according to strict tradition, often passed down through generations of family stall-owners.

Street food brings people together, as folk crowd onto their neighbourhood streets to share meals and conversation at their favourite stall. Some vendors operate in the same spot for decades, giving a sense of continuation that can span several generations. And while Asian cities modernise at a rampant pace, with glimmering malls replacing gritty old laneways and younger generations becoming wealthier and more sophisticated by the nanosecond, street eating isn't going anywhere yet. It continues to cut across age, gender, religion, economic status and every other demography you'd care to mention. It's at the core of the very fabric of cities like Bangkok, Kuala Lumpur, Jakarta and Saigon, making visits to these place just one giant excuse to eat amazingly good food, outdoors.

In this book, I want to take you with me as I delve into the street food scenes that thrive across some of my all-time favourite Asian cities. You'll find full recipes, as well as stories about some of the amazing dishes I came across on my travels, and where you can find them when you visit. Even if you can't be there in person, you can still create the smells, sounds, energy and flavours at home, in your very own kitchen, by cooking these recipes. I hope also that when you read about the vendors and street food cooks that have become special to me, and from whom I have learned so much, you'll be inspired to seek them out when you do find yourself in Bangkok or Jakarta, Kuala Lumpur or Saigon. Eating their food, in situ, is the best kind of culinary travel experience you could possibly have.

VISIT
SAIGON
VIETNAM

(SAIGON) 10 PM
VĨNH KHÁNH STREET
DISTRICT 4

Saigon. Crazy-hectic and developing at an astounding pace, it's got an energy and dynamism you can almost smell. I totally love it. Maybe I'm biased though, as the city is now my second home. It's also where my family came from before they moved to Australia all those years ago, so the place is virtually in my DNA.

Naturally I'm addicted to the street food, and I practically trip over it every day because this town is one heaving smorgasbord of outdoor dining options, wherever you venture or look. Seafood, fresh herbs, prodigious varieties of vegetables, sweetish, light flavours, and simple cooking styles are the hallmarks of Saigon's food, though being Vietnam's biggest city, there's plenty of regional fare from other corners of the country on offer too. Throw in some French influence (you haven't lived until you've had Vietnamese drip coffee with condensed milk, or a crunchy-fluffy baguette filled with local charcuterie) and an uber-vibrant Chinatown and you've got an incredibly rich street food repertoire.

The locals all have their favourite food haunts and one of mine is Cô Giang Street in District 1. I like to come here early, when it's still a little calm, and breakfast on bún thịt nướng, which consists of honey-marinated grilled pork, springy rice noodles, herbs, pickled vegetables, spring rolls and peanuts. This dish, typical of Saigon cuisine, contains every texture imaginable – crunchy, slippery, chewy, snappy, slurpy.

During the day, as I poke around streets and back alleys across Saigon's 24 districts, I can't stop grazing on tasty little snacks. Like bánh khọt: crisp, soft-centred 'pancakes' made in special pans using a turmeric-scented batter. You eat them with fresh herbs, wrapped in lettuce leaves and dipped in nuoc cham, or sweetened fish sauce. Then there are Saigon's myriad soups, which are perfect for this hot climate. Súp cua óc heo, or crab soup with pork brain, is light and fragrant and way more delicious than it might sound. Bún mắm is a porky-seafoody noodle soup dish based on pungent, fermented anchovy stock that's really typical of this part of Vietnam, and another favourite dish. And, of course, there's phở. When people ask where I get the best phở (and they always do), I take them down an alleyway in District 1, through clouds of spice-infused steam, where the family at Phở Ngoc have been making this iconic dish for 40 years. Coming here is like being fed by your grandmother; the atmosphere is warm and the phở is indescribably good.

As night settles, the pace on the street intensifies, with scooters, cyclists and taxis zeroing in on favourite evening eats. I like to hang out in non-touristy District 4, where my uncle lives. The fragrance of lemongrass, lime, black pepper and garlic oil hangs in the air and there's cooking – and eating – activity right on the pavements. Uncle Four has shown me all his special haunts and now, if you come with me, I'll share them with you too.

SERVES 4

2 tablespoons sugar

4 tablespoons fish sauce

1 tablespoon honey

1 teaspoon freshly ground black pepper

6 spring onions (scallions), white parts thinly sliced, plus a few green ends, sliced, to garnish

2 garlic cloves, finely diced

500 g (1 lb 2 oz) pork neck, thinly cut across the grain into 3 mm (⅛ in) thick slices

2 tablespoons vegetable oil

VERMICELLI NOODLE SALAD

250 g (9 oz) rice vermicelli noodles, cooked according to packet instructions

5 mint leaves, roughly sliced

5 perilla leaves (see glossary), roughly sliced

5 Vietnamese mint leaves, roughly sliced

1 Lebanese (short) cucumber, halved lengthways and sliced

2 handfuls bean sprouts

125 ml (4 fl oz/½ cup) Nuoc Cham (see page 90)

4 tablespoons Spring Onion Oil (see page 91)

4 tablespoons Fried Red Asian Shallots (see page 152)

4 tablespoons crushed roasted peanuts

CHARGRILLED PORK SKEWERS WITH VERMICELLI NOODLE SALAD

BÚN THỊT NƯỚNG

Cô Giang Street in Saigon's District 1 is hands-down one of my favourite food streets. As you walk down it, you can see and smell clouds of rich aroma percolating in the air. Where it crosses with Đề Thám Street is my go-to place for this noodle dish, one of the few Vietnamese noodle dishes to be eaten without a broth but, instead, with the popular Vietnamese dipping sauce nuoc cham, and lots of it too – enough to immerse the vermicelli and the fresh herbs. The pork skewers, which are traditionally made up on lemongrass stems, are chargrilled over charcoal, and the aromas of the lemongrass and the herbs are bewitching.

In a large mixing bowl, combine the sugar, fish sauce, honey and pepper. Mix until the sugar has dissolved.

Pound the white parts of the spring onions to a paste using a mortar and pestle, then add to the bowl with the garlic and pork. Toss to coat the pork well, then pour over the vegetable oil. Cover and marinate in the refrigerator for 2 hours, or overnight for an even tastier result.

When you're nearly ready to cook, soak 12 bamboo skewers in water for 20 minutes to prevent scorching. Once marinated, thread the pork onto the skewers, discarding the remaining marinade.

Heat a chargrill pan or barbecue chargrill to medium–high. Chargrill the pork skewers, for 1–2 minutes on each side, or until the meat is cooked through and nicely browned.

Divide the noodles between four serving bowls. Top with the herbs, cucumber and bean sprouts, then sit the pork skewers on top.

Drizzle over the nuoc cham and spring onion oil. Sprinkle with the fried shallots, crushed peanuts and green spring onion slices.

**Chinese
Doughnuts**
Giò Cháo Quẩy

30 >

**Mini Rice
Flour Pockets
with Tiger
Prawns &
Prawn Floss**
Bánh Khọt

MAKES 12

450 g (1 lb) plain (all-purpose) flour
⅓ teaspoon sugar
1 teaspoon baking powder
⅓ teaspoon bicarbonate of soda
    (baking soda)
vegetable oil, for deep-frying
sea salt

CHINESE DOUGHNUTS

GIÒ CHÁO QUẨY

From the name you'll be able to guess that this dish originates in China, where it is typically eaten with congee for breakfast. In Saigon, these doughnuts are eaten either on their own or also with congee, while in the north of the country the locals enjoy theirs with a bowl of steaming phở. Crunchy on the outside, soft and doughy on the inside, they make a great snack.

Put the flour in a large bowl. Make a well in the middle and pour 250 ml (9 fl oz/ 1 cup) water into it, then add the sugar, baking powder, bicarbonate of soda and a pinch of sea salt. Mix all the ingredients together, then knead to form a soft, smooth dough either by hand or in a mixer fitted with a dough hook. Cover the dough with a tea towel (dish towel) and leave to rest in a warm place for about 30 minutes.

Cover a baking sheet in a layer of plastic wrap.

Turn the rested dough out onto a clean, lightly floured surface and knead for a further 1–2 minutes. Shape the dough into a flat loaf about 60 cm (24 in) long, 10 cm (4 in) wide and 1.5 cm (⅝ in) thick, taking the time to make it truly uniform. Place the dough in the centre of the prepared baking sheet and wrap it up in the plastic wrap, tucking the ends of the plastic under the loaf, and ensuring that the dough is completely covered. Cover with an extra layer of plastic wrap, transfer to the refrigerator and leave to rest for at least 7 hours, or overnight.

Once rested, remove the dough from the refrigerator and leave it for 2 hours to reach room temperature, then cut it crossways into 1.5 cm (⅝ in) strips.

Divide the strips into pairs, placing one strip on top of the other. Using the back of your knife or a chopstick, press a line through the centre of each pair of strips without cutting all the way through (this will help shape the doughnuts).

Half-fill a wok or large saucepan with vegetable oil and heat to 180°C (350°F), or until a cube of bread dropped into the oil browns in 15 seconds. Lower the dough pieces into the hot oil, in batches if necessary, and fry for 1–2 minutes, turning them every 30 seconds, until golden brown and puffy. Remove the doughnuts with tongs or chopsticks and drain on paper towel before serving.

MINI RICE FLOUR POCKETS WITH TIGER PRAWNS & PRAWN FLOSS

BÁNH KHỌT

Next on my Cô Giang food crawl menu is this fantastic dish – a miniature version of the typical Vietnamese savoury pancakes (bánh xèo), traditionally eaten with lettuce cups or mustard leaves, fresh herbs and pickled veggies before being dunked in nuoc cham. These little pancakes are often cooked in a special cast-iron griddle pan over a high heat, which leaves the outside texture crispy while keeping the insides creamy and soft.

Half-fill a steamer, wok or large saucepan with water and bring to a rapid boil over a high heat.

Line a steamer basket or bamboo steamer with baking paper and punch a few small holes in the paper. Drain the mung beans and place them in the steamer, then set over the pan and cover with a lid. Steam for 15 minutes, or until the beans are soft. Set aside.

To make the prawn floss, use a mortar and pestle to pound the diced prawns to a smooth paste.

Place a small non-stick saucepan over a low heat, add the prawn paste and cook for 20–30 minutes, stirring the mixture regularly and pressing it down onto the bottom of the pan using the back of a fork, until the prawn meat is dry, fibrous and crisp. (The idea is to dry the prawn meat — it should not colour, and you should notice a small amount of steam being released from the prawns.) Remove from the heat and leave to cool to room temperature.

For the batter, combine the rice flour, turmeric and a pinch of salt in a bowl and mix well. Add 250 ml (9 fl oz/1 cup) water, the coconut cream and the cooked rice and stir to combine, then blend until smooth with a hand-held blender.

Slice the whole prawns in half lengthways, then slice each half into three pieces and set aside.

Heat an eight-mould bánh khọt pan or a Dutch pancake pan (poffertjes pan) over a medium–high heat and brush the moulds with vegetable oil. Add a tablespoon of batter to each mould, turning the pan in a circular motion to run the batter up the edges of the moulds, then add a pinch each of steamed mung bean and sliced spring onion together with a few prawn pieces to each mould. Place the lid over the pan, reduce the heat slightly and cook for 2–3 minutes, or until the batter is cooked through.

Using a teaspoon, remove the pockets from the moulds and transfer to a serving platter. Repeat the cooking process with any leftover batter and prawns.

To serve, sprinkle a generous amount of the prawn floss over each pocket and drizzle with spring onion oil and nuoc cham.

MAKES 8

1 tablespoon dried mung beans, soaked in cold water overnight
4 cooked tiger prawns (shrimp), peeled and deveined
vegetable oil, for brushing
1 spring onion (scallion), green part only, thinly sliced
60 ml (2 fl oz/¼ cup) Spring Onion Oil (see page 91), for drizzling
60 ml (2 fl oz/¼ cup) Nuoc Cham (see page 90), for drizzling

PRAWN FLOSS

6 cooked tiger prawns (shrimp), peeled, deveined and finely diced

BATTER

125 g (4½ oz) rice flour
¼ teaspoon ground turmeric
50 ml (2 fl oz) coconut cream
60 g (2¼ oz/⅓ cup) left-over cooked jasmine rice
sea salt

FISHCAKE BAGUETTE

BÁNH MÌ CHẢ CÁ	Cô Giang Market, District 1	VND 15,000 AUD $1.00

If you look out onto the streets of Saigon in the early morning – or indeed anywhere across Vietnam – you will likely spot a woman in a conical hat, pushing her food cart to its destination. There, she brings out the kilos and kilos of fishcakes that she has prepared the night before and begins to deep-fry them in her large wok, where they slowly puff up and float in the oil like fluffy clouds. Vietnamese fishcakes are usually chewy and are best served hot, so once cooked, they are sliced up and piled into soft, fresh baguettes with cucumber, chilli, soy sauce and perhaps a drizzle or two of chilli sauce for a little extra kick.

SHREDDED PORK BAGUETTE

BÁNH MÌ BÌ	Cô Giang Street, District 1	VND 15,000 AUD $1.00

This shredded pork baguette is a much-loved snack in Saigon, though it is not often seen outside of Vietnam. To the eye it looks like the warm, crisp baguette is filled with a mixture of shredded pork and clear glass noodles, but a closer inspection reveals the 'noodles' are actually pig's skin that has been pressure-cooked and then sliced into thin strips. The skin is then tossed with the shredded pork and a generous amount of toasted rice powder, which provides a lovely contrast of texture, before being slipped into the baguettes.

PORK & MUSHROOM BALLS WITH VERMICELLI NOODLES (PORK PEPPER BALL SOUP)

BÚN MỌC	71 Đề Thám Street, District 1	VND 25,000 AUD $1.50

Originally from northern Vietnam, bún mọc is a Vietnamese noodle soup dish unlike any other. The broth, made of pork bones and shiitake mushrooms, is clean and simple in flavour with a strong, peppery taste, though the highlight of the dish is undoubtedly the pork balls – spoonfuls of minced (ground) pork that are added to the hot broth to cook. While there are stalls that offer these little balls deep-fried, I much prefer them cooked this way, as they have the chance to absorb the flavours of the stock. Once the pork balls are cooked, the soup is then ladled into bowls and enjoyed with rice vermicelli noodles, fresh banana blossom and a selection of fresh herbs. The light, earthy scented soup makes a great breakfast dish and can be found all around Saigon, though my go-to is a little store at 71 Đề Thám Street in District 1. Here, the vendor changes their dishes every day of the week (bún mọc is available on Saturdays) and I always sit across the road because the store is so busy – they only have a few stools out the front along a bench and they're always taken. From here I get to observe the hum of the motorbikes, cycles and daily hustle and bustle of the nearby market, before the vendor weaves across the busy road with my tray of hot noodles, sauces, side salads and fresh herbs. It's a perfect place to watch city life rush by.

OFFAL CONGEE

CHÁO LÒNG

**Cháo Lòng Bà Út,
Cô Giang Street, District 1**

VND 25,000 AUD $1.50

On Cô Giang Street in District 1 I head towards Cháo Lòng Bà Út, one of the oldest street stalls in Saigon. Grandma Ut (the owner) tells me that she inherited the business from her mother and has been cooking for over 60 years, starting out on the streets before setting up a stall at the present location on District 1's Cô Giang Street in 1975. Though nowadays when you visit you will find her niece Chin running the business, occasionally you'll see Grandma Ut helping out or mingling with the regular customers. So what has attracted so many generations of locals, including myself, you might ask? The answer is her simply irresistible cháo lòng, stuffed pork intestines served in a flavourful rice porridge made with steaming pork stock and fresh blood jelly. Although the exact details of Grandma Ut's recipe are a closely guarded secret, she reveals that she uses shin bones and the juices from boiling the offal – including the intestines, heart, kidney and stomach – to give the congee its delicate sweetness. The offal itself is stuffed with minced (ground) pork, handfuls of fresh soft herbs, perilla leaves (see glossary), spices and bone marrow and steamed before being deep-fried until nicely golden brown. It is served with Chinese doughnuts (see page 30) to soak up the delicious juices, a moreish sweet and sour fish sauce for dipping and lots of bean sprouts and lime chunks.

SERVES 8

2 kg (4 lb 8 oz) oxtail, cut into 3 cm
(1¼ in) pieces (ask your butcher
to do this for you)
4 tablespoons sea salt
5 large onions, 4 whole plus
1 finely sliced
150 g (5½ oz) piece unpeeled
fresh ginger
1 x 1 kg (2 lb 4 oz) boneless
beef brisket
190 ml (6½ fl oz/¾ cup) fish sauce
80 g (3 oz) rock sugar (see glossary)
or granulated sugar
1.6 kg (3 lb 8 oz) fresh rice noodles
400 g (14 oz) trimmed beef sirloin,
thinly sliced
4 spring onions (scallions), sliced
coriander (cilantro) sprigs, to garnish
2 bird's eye chillies, sliced
1 lime, cut into wedges
freshly ground black pepper

SPICE POUCH

8 whole cloves
5 star anise
2 cassia bark sticks, each about
10 cm (3½ in) in length
1 tablespoon black peppercorns

TO SERVE

bean sprouts
Thai basil
saw-tooth coriander (cilantro;
see glossary)
hoisin sauce
sriracha chilli sauce

BEEF NOODLE SOUP

PHỞ BO

Two questions I am often asked are, 'what is "phở"?' and, 'where does it come from?' To answer the second, though the exact origins are unclear, rumour has it that phở was created in North Vietnam in the early 20th century. Both Chinese and French cooking heavily influenced the dish, which may have been derived from the French beef stew 'pot-au-feu'. A hearty, broth-based noodle soup often made with beef or chicken, it varies from region to region. In northern Vietnam the broth is likely to be lighter and made with fewer ingredients, the noodles served with thin beef slices and ginger, or chicken and lime leaves, and accompanied by bean sprouts, herbs, lime and fresh chilli on the side. In southern Vietnam, the broth is a lot sweeter and made from more ingredients, and the accompaniments also include hoisin sauce, fish sauce and chilli paste.

To get my phở fix in Saigon, I visit District 1's Phở Ngọc on Hồ Hảo Hớn Street, which has been running for over 30 years. The diners are regular customers – I meet a man who tells me his grandma has been eating here since she could remember and that she brings him here every Saturday as a family ritual. Add a poached egg to the broth when ordering for extra silkiness.

Put the oxtail in a large saucepan and pour over enough cold water to submerge it. Add 3 tablespoons of the salt and leave to soak for 1 hour, then drain.

To prepare the spice pouch, toast each spice separately in a dry frying pan over a medium heat until fragrant. Allow the spices to cool, then pound them into a coarse powder using a mortar and pestle. Add the ground spices to a 40 cm (16 in) square of muslin (cheesecloth) and tie up tightly in a knot. Set aside.

Heat a chargrill pan or barbecue grill to medium–high. Cook the whole onions and ginger for 15 minutes, turning regularly, until blackened on all sides. Leave to cool, then remove and discard the blackened skins and chop the flesh.

Put the oxtail, brisket and 6 litres (210 fl oz/24 cups) cold water in a stockpot, bring to the boil and cook for 15 minutes, constantly skimming any impurities off the surface (this will ensure a clean, clear broth). Reduce the heat to a slow simmer and add the fish sauce, remaining 1 tablespoon salt, rock sugar, chopped onion and ginger, and the spice pouch. Cover and simmer for 3 hours, or until the stock has reduced by almost half.

Strain the stock through a piece of muslin. Remove the brisket and set aside to cool, then thinly slice. Return the stock to the pot and keep warm.

Bring a saucepan of water to a simmer. Divide the noodles into eight portions. Blanch each portion of noodles separately in the simmering water for 5 seconds, then drain and transfer to serving bowls.

Place three or four slices of brisket on top of the noodles in each bowl, followed by three or four slices of raw sirloin. Pour over the hot stock to cover the noodles and beef, then top each bowl with the sliced onion and spring onion. Season with freshly ground black pepper and garnish with coriander sprigs.

Add the chilli slices and a squeeze of lime to each bowl and serve with bean sprouts, Thai basil, saw-tooth coriander and an even mixture of hoisin sauce and sriracha chilli sauce for dipping the meat slices into.

At Phở Ngọc, the cooks put on a real show as they blanch the noodles, throwing them high into the air before catching them in a bowl.

VIETNAMESE STEAMED RICE ROLLS WITH A PORK & MUSHROOM STUFFING

BÁNH CUỐN

MAKES 12

2 tablespoons vegetable oil,
   plus extra for brushing
2 garlic cloves, diced
4 red Asian shallots, diced
300 g (10½ oz) minced (ground) pork
4 fresh black fungus (wood ears;
   see glossary), thinly sliced
1 teaspoon fish sauce
½ teaspoon sugar
1 bunch perilla (see glossary),
   leaves picked
1 bunch Vietnamese mint,
   leaves picked
1 bunch mint, leaves picked
2 handfuls bean sprouts
2 tablespoons Fried Red Asian
   Shallots (see page 152)
2 Lebanese (short) cucumbers,
   sliced into batons
250 ml (9 fl oz/1 cup) Nuoc Cham
   (see page 90)
2 red bird's eye chillies, sliced
sea salt
freshly ground black pepper

BATTER

200 g (7 oz) rice flour
60 g (2¼ oz/½ cup) tapioca flour
½ teaspoon sea salt
½ teaspoon vegetable oil

Beautiful, elegant to eat and amazing to watch being prepared, bánh cuốn is one of my all-time favourite Vietnamese breakfast dishes. The delicate rice flour sheets can be made extremely thin and I love to watch the aunties making these. To start, they slowly pour a very thin layer of the rice batter onto a fabric-covered pot and evenly spread it paper thin, then cover it briefly with a lid to cook. Less than a minute later, the delicate rice flour wrappers are picked up using a flat bamboo stick and transferred to their boards. They are then filled with stir-fried pork and mushrooms and carefully rolled. Topped with fresh herbs and served with warm nuoc cham, breakfast doesn't come much tastier than this.

For the batter, add the ingredients to a mixing bowl with 600 ml (20 fl oz/2½ cups) cold water and whisk until smooth. Cover with plastic wrap and leave to rest for 20 minutes.

Heat a wok over a medium heat. Add the vegetable oil and sauté the garlic and shallots for 30 seconds, or until fragrant. Add the pork, mushrooms, fish sauce, sugar and a pinch of sea salt and black pepper. Stir-fry for 4 minutes, then transfer to a bowl and set aside.

Brush a round tray with vegetable oil and set it next to the stovetop. Heat a 20 cm (8 in) non-stick crêpe pan over a low heat and brush it with oil. Pour 3 tablespoons of the batter into the pan, moving it quickly in a circular motion to cover the base evenly with a thin layer (the thinner the better!). Cover with a lid and cook for 45 seconds, then slide the thin noodle sheet onto the oiled tray. Repeat this process using the remaining batter, adding more oil to the pan as necessary.

To assemble the rolls, scoop 1 tablespoon of the pork mixture onto the centre of a noodle sheet, then fold it over to form an open-ended roll. Transfer to a serving plate and repeat with the remaining filling and noodle sheets.

To serve, top the rolls with the herbs, bean sprouts, fried shallots and cucumber. Drizzle over the nuoc cham and scatter over the chilli.

ROAST PORK, LING & FERMENTED ANCHOVY BROTH WITH RICE NOODLES

BÚN MẮM

Bến Thành Market, District 1

VND 25,000 AUD $1.50

I really love this unique noodle soup – a must-try dish with a broth made from pungent, fermented anchovy stock and served with roast pork, chunky fish pieces, prawns (shrimp), calamari and eggplant (aubergine). I like ordering this from a place opposite the east gate of District 1's bustling Bến Thành Market. This little shop-house has been running for over 45 years. Their prices are higher than others nearby, however they use premium produce to create their specialty noodle soup and it's money well spent.

CRAB & TOMATO BROTH WITH VERMICELLI NOODLES

BÚN RIÊU	Phan Bội Châu Street, District 1	VND 30,000 AUD $1.75

Vietnam is a land of noodle soups. The locals enjoy at least one bowl of noodles a day and there are noodle soups to be eaten for breakfast, lunch and dinner. For me, lunch-time noodles means one dish, bún riêu, a classic crab and tomato broth noodle soup originally from northern Vietnam – the rusty red colour of the tomato broth, coloured with annatto seeds, is unlike any other. Freshwater paddy crabs are ground into a paste and boiled in the broth into soft crab cakes, while in the south you will find fried tofu and pig's blood jelly included. I like to eat mine from a place on District 1's Phan Bội Châu Street, where they also add shrimp paste and tamarind juice to give it that extra kick. They finish it off with fresh banana blossom, shredded water spinach (morning glory), sliced chilli and blanched bean sprouts.

SILKWORM NOODLES WITH SHREDDED PORK & COCONUT MILK

BÁNH TẰM BÌ	Trần Đình Xu Street Market, District 1	VND 25,000 AUD $1.50

This is a popular dish in Saigon and across southern Vietnam, though it is not easily found outside of the country. The thick noodles – which resemble silkworms, hence the name – are made from a combination of rice flour and tapioca flour. Coated in a thick, coconut milk sauce, they are drizzled with generous quantities of Nuoc Cham (see page 90) and served with shredded pork and pork skin, cooked bean sprouts, julienned cucumbers, fresh herbs, pickled vegetables and Spring Onion Oil (see page 91). Both sweet and savoury, somewhere in between an entrée and dessert, I love to enjoy it as an afternoon pick-me-up treat!

CRAB & TAPIOCA NOODLE SOUP

BÁNH CANH CUA

Phan Bội Châu Street, District 1

VND 70,000 AUD $4.50

This thick and slippery tapioca noodle soup originated in South Vietnam and is still not widely known across the country – in fact, I have quite a few friends from the North who have never heard of this noodle dish before. I like to eat it in District 1 at a place on Phan Bội Châu Street across from the busy Bến Thành Market, where it features crab, cubes of pig's blood jelly, prawns (shrimp) and quail eggs, and is garnished with spring onions (scallions) and coriander (cilantro). The udon-like texture of the chewy, soft tapioca flour noodles always leaves me craving more.

CRISPY SKIN CHICKEN WITH RED RICE

GÀ XỐI MỠ

55 Tú Xương Street, District 3

VND 40,000   AUD $2.50

We serve this dish at my Red Lantern restaurant in Sydney. We poach the chicken in a master stock, then baste it with a honey and maltose mixture before hanging it until the skin becomes completely dry. To then achieve a very crispy skin, we ladle very hot oil over the skin again and again until it blisters and becomes crispy. The whole process is very time-consuming, but is well worth it, so when I come across this place at 55 Tú Xương Street in District 3 I am blown away. Here, instead of ladling the hot oil over his chicken, the owner-cook has built his own fryer that showers hot oil over the meat. It's absolute genius. The sauce served with the chicken is top secret. However, after tasting it, I can tell you it is a blend of oyster sauce, soy sauce, hoisin sauce, garlic and chilli. It's delicious served with the red rice, too.

STICKY RICE WITH CHICKEN

XÔI GÀ	15 Nguyễn Trung Trực Street, District 1	VND 30,000 AUD $1.75

Stumbling past this extremely busy little store in District 1 on my way to a café one afternoon, I run into a queue 20 people deep. Intrigued, I see their specialty written up simply as 'Sticky Rice with Chicken' and, while waiting for my dish, I notice there's another sticky rice with chicken store located right next door, with the exact same name 'Xôi Gà Number 1'. To kill my curiosity, I ask the staff if it is owned by the same person and find out that the original owner worked here for 25 years after previously selling her rice around the neighbourhood on the street. Becoming ill, she passed the business on to one of her daughters and her other daughter, angry that she didn't inherit the business, decided to open her own sticky rice shop right next door! Be sure you go to the original, located at 15 Nguyễn Trung Trực Street. Make sure you order chicken sticky rice with THE LOT, which will comprise of sticky rice, shredded chicken, lap cheong (see glossary), chicken giblets, oocyte (immature eggs), and pickled daikon (white radish) and carrots.

BAGUETTE FILLED WITH CHARGRILLED PORK PATTIES

BÁNH MÌ THỊT NƯỚNG	Hẻm 39 Nguyễn Trãi, District 1	VND 15,000 AUD $1.00

I remember being introduced to this by a close friend of mine, who said that, if pressed to pick the best bánh mì vendor in Saigon, she would definitely say this one. The hidden cart is located down a narrow alleyway, Hẻm 39 Nguyễn Trãi, right in the middle of District 1, where the hawker starts selling from 4.30 pm until she finishes all her baguettes (usually around 7 pm). Be prepared to queue when here, and don't be surprised when you see people ordering bags and bags full. Oh and don't be shy to scream out what you want, because even though there's a queue, it doesn't necessarily mean it's your turn. Believe me, you don't want to miss out on your chance of grabbing one of Saigon's tastiest baguettes.

So what makes this particular bánh mì so popular? What I love about it is that the vendor doesn't over pack her baguettes, leaving just enough room to taste all the flavours that have been stuffed inside. The pork patty or 'nem nướng' is chargrilled to perfection and is still very juicy in the centre. To it she adds fresh coriander (cilantro) and cucumber with pickled carrot and daikon (white radish) before drizzling over her 'secret sauce', with its sweet, salty flavour and decent hit of ground chilli. It sure is one of the finest bánh mì thịt nướng in town.

VIETNAMESE PORK BAGUETTE

BÁNH MÌ THỊT	Bánh Mì Huynh Hoa, Lê Thị Riêng Street, District 1	VND 35,000 AUD $2.00

Bánh mì is a great example of the French influence on Vietnamese cuisine, and is known to be one of the best sandwiches in the world. 'Where's the best Vietnamese pork roll in Saigon?', I am always asked. Now, there are hundreds of great bánh mì carts in Saigon, but my favourite would have to be Bánh Mì Huynh Hoa on Lê Thị Riêng Street by the Bến Thành Market in District 1. The store is also known by another name, 'Bánh Mì O Moi' which translates as 'lesbian baguette' – the reason being that the store was opened by a lesbian couple and was originally staffed by an all-lesbian workforce. The pair still run the store and they are true artisans – their baguettes are freshly baked and kept warm in a charcoal-fuelled oven, while their pâtés and cold cuts are divine. Be sure to get there around opening at 3.30 pm to avoid the long queues and make sure you ask for pork floss on your bánh mì.

BẢNG GIÁ
1 ổ   33.000
2 ổ   66.000
3 ổ   99.000
4 ổ   132.000
5 ổ   165.000
6 ổ   198.000
7 ổ   231.000
8 ổ   264.000
9 ổ   297.000
10 ổ   330.000

KHÁCH HÀNG KIỂM TIỀN
TRƯỚC KHI RỜI QUẦY

BÁNH MÌ
33.000đ/ 1 ổ

RICE PAPER & GREEN MANGO SALAD

BÁNH TRÁNG TRỘN

Notre Dame Cathedral, District 1

VND 15,000 AUD $1.00

By Notre Dame Cathedral in District 1 you'll find numerous vendors selling this speedy snack beloved by the city's teenagers. Unlike most fast food, however, this is actually really healthy and good for you as well as being rather uniquely served; it's dished up in a small plastic bag, with the idea being that you toss the ingredients together yourself by shaking the bag before eating straight from it. So into the bag go peanuts, fried shallots, strips of tart green mango, salty dried shrimp (see glossary), beef jerky, boiled quail eggs, strips of rice paper and fresh herbs, including Vietnamese mint and saw-tooth coriander (cilantro; see glossary). The resulting jumble delivers a salad where each mouthful bursts with awesome flavours and textures.

CHARGRILLED RICE PAPER WITH QUAIL EGG & DRIED SHRIMP

BÁNH TRÁNG NƯỚNG	Notre Dame Cathedral, District 1	VND 15,000 AUD $1.00

I only discovered this dish a few years ago, when I spotted the street food vendors firing up their grills across the road from the Notre Dame Cathedral in District 1. Originally from Da Lat in Central Vietnam, it's very popular among young students as it's cheap and delicious – I call it Vietnamese pizza. To make it, rice paper is grilled over charcoal, a quail egg is then cracked and spread over the top before the surface is sprinkled with minced (ground) pork, spring onions (scallions) and dried shrimp (see glossary). A decent drizzle of sriracha chilli sauce adds that final hit of flavour.

CRAB & PIG'S BRAIN SOUP

SÚP CUA ÓC HEO

8 asparagus spears, trimmed
1 tablespoon vegetable oil
1 red Asian shallot, thinly sliced
100 g (3½ oz) pig's brain, cleaned
    and cut into 5 mm (¼ in) cubes
200 g (7 oz) cooked crabmeat
200 g (7 oz) enoki mushrooms,
    trimmed and separated
1 teaspoon sea salt
1.5 litres (54 fl oz/6 cups)
    Fish Stock (see page 91)
2 tablespoons fish sauce
2 tablespoons potato starch, dissolved
    in 125 ml (4 fl oz/½ cup) water
2 spring onions (scallions),
    thinly sliced

TO SERVE
light soy sauce
chilli oil
sesame oil
½ teaspoon ground white pepper
2 tablespoons chopped coriander
    (cilantro) leaves

This dish reminds me of attending Vietnamese and Chinese weddings with my family as a child; the first dish served would invariably be a chicken and corn soup, thickened using cornflour (cornstarch). This very Chinese-influenced soup is similar in spirit and you find it all over Saigon, sold from little carts; the brains definitely make it a local favourite. Plus, it's probably one of the cheaper street food dishes, even though it contains tip-top ingredients like crab, asparagus, enoki mushrooms and, of course, those brains. Sometimes the cooks put quail eggs in it too. It's a very straightforward dish to make at home and I hope you try it. You can get the fresh pig's brains from any Asian butcher.

Bring a saucepan of water to the boil. Add the asparagus and blanch for 2 minutes. Drain, refresh in iced water to stop the cooking process, then drain again. Cut the blanched asparagus crossways into thin slices and set aside.

Heat the oil in a saucepan over a medium heat. Add the shallot and cook for 2–3 minutes, or until softened. Add the cubed brain, asparagus, crabmeat, enoki mushrooms and salt and cook, stirring, for 2 minutes, until just tender. Set aside.

Bring the fish stock to a slow simmer in a stockpot or large saucepan. Add the fish sauce and potato starch liquid and stir until the broth thickens, then stir in the brain mixture and the spring onions and simmer for a further 2 minutes.

Divide the soup between 4–6 serving bowls, adding a dash of soy sauce, chilli oil and sesame oil and a sprinkle of white pepper to each. Garnish with the coriander and serve.

RICE PAPER ROLLS WITH GRILLED LEMONGRASS BEEF BETEL LEAVES & STAR FRUIT

BÒ CUỐN LÁ LỐT BÁNH TRÁNG

80 g (3 oz) rice vermicelli noodles, cooked according to packet instructions
1 bunch perilla (see glossary), leaves picked
1 bunch Vietnamese mint
1 Lebanese (short) cucumber, cut into batons
2 star fruit (carambola; see glossary), thinly sliced
60 ml (2 fl oz/¼ cup) Nuoc Cham (see page 90), for dipping
20 x 22 cm (8½ in) rice paper sheets
finely chopped bird's eye chillies, to serve

GRILLED LEMONGRASS BEEF BETEL LEAVES

400 g (14 oz) minced (ground) beef
2 lemongrass stems, white part only, finely chopped
4 spring onions (scallions), white part only, finely chopped
1 garlic clove, finely chopped
2 teaspoons sea salt
2 teaspoons ground white pepper
1 bunch betel leaves (see glossary)
vegetable oil, for brushing

On Cô Giang Street in District 1 there is a guy who cooks this dish using just a basic chargrill. Betel leaves are interesting; where the Thais like theirs raw, the Vietnamese love to cook them either in stir-fries or stuffed and chargrilled, as here. The stuffing is a mixture of minced beef, lemongrass, garlic, fish sauce and coriander; it's rolled neatly in the leaves to make small, tight rolls, which are then grilled. You can eat these little packages in lots of ways; stuffed into baguettes, for example. But my favourite is to wrap them in rice paper with fresh vermicelli noodles, tons of fresh herbs and some star fruit and green banana (although I've left this out of my recipe), for a slightly sour edge. This is a ripper of a dish to cook for a barbecue at home.

For the beef betel leaves, combine the beef, lemongrass, spring onions, garlic, salt and white pepper in a mixing bowl. Cover and allow the flavours to infuse for at least 15 minutes.

Meanwhile, remove the stems from the individual betel leaves and wash the leaves in cold water. Lay flat on a cloth to dry.

Once dry, lay a large betel leaf (or two smaller leaves), shiny side down, on a chopping board with the stem end of the leaf pointing towards you. Spoon approximately 1 tablespoon of the beef mixture onto the bottom edge of the leaf. Work the mixture into a sausage shape using your hands, then roll the leaf from bottom to top, folding in the sides to enclose the meat and form a parcel. Place the parcel, seam side down, on your chopping board to stop the leaf unrolling. Repeat this process until you have used all of the beef.

Heat a chargrill pan or barbecue chargrill to medium. Brush the betel leaf parcels with oil, arrange them, seam side down, and grill for about 5 minutes, turning to colour all over, until cooked through.

Arrange the vermicelli noodles, fresh herbs, cucumber, star fruit and cooked betel leaves on a large round tray. Pour the nuoc cham into 4-6 small dipping bowls, then allow your guests to wrap and roll their own rice paper rolls. To assemble one, dip a rice paper sheet into a bowl of water, then lay it flat on a plate. Place two cooked betel leaf parcels in the centre of the sheet crossways, approximately 4 cm (1½ in) from the top. Below the betel leaf parcels add some of the perilla leaves, Vietnamese mint, vermicelli, cucumber and star fruit. Fold the sides into the centre over the filling, then roll the bottom of the paper up to form a tight roll. Repeat with the remaining ingredients.

SERVES 4–6 AS AN ENTRÉE OR SNACK

CENTRAL-STYLE PANCAKES

BÁNH XÈO MIỀN TRUNG

50 g (1¾ oz) dried mung beans,
    soaked overnight then drained
2 tablespoons vegetable oil
1 garlic clove, chopped
400 g (14 oz) raw school prawns
    (shrimp) or other small prawns,
    shell on
200 g (7 oz) boneless pork belly,
    fat trimmed and thinly sliced
1 spring onion (scallion), thinly sliced
50 g (1¾ oz) bean sprouts
pinch of sea salt and ground
    white pepper

PANCAKE BATTER
80 g (2¾ oz/½ cup) rice flour
20 g (¾ oz) plain (all-purpose) flour
½ teaspoon sea salt
1 teaspoon ground turmeric
160 ml (5½ fl oz) coconut cream
160 ml (5½ fl oz) chilled soda water
1 spring onion (scallion), thinly sliced

TO SERVE
12 mustard green leaves
    (see glossary)
1 handful perilla leaves (see glossary)
1 handful mint leaves
100 ml (3½ fl oz) Nuoc Cham
    (see page 90), for dipping

'Bánh xèo' literally means 'sizzling' in Vietnamese; when you pour the batter into a hot pan it sizzles madly, hence the name. In the central part of the country, the bánh xèo are much smaller than they are in Saigon – and my guy on Cô Giang Street makes this dainty-sized one. The batter is made using regular flour, rice flour, turmeric and coconut cream and the secret to crisp, crusty, crunchy bánh xèo is to cook them in quite a hot pan. On the street, they use copious amounts of oil but they get crisp just as well in a non-stick pan with minimal oil. Inside the bánh xèo are prawns, bits of pork, bean sprouts and cooked mung beans and, to eat the pancake, which is served folded over, you wrap large pieces of it together with fresh herbs in rice paper and lettuce leaves and dunk it into nuoc cham. It's one of my all-time favourite things to eat; I just love it.

Half-fill a wok or large saucepan with water and bring to a rapid boil over a high heat.

Line a steamer basket or bamboo steamer with baking paper and punch a few small holes in the paper. Drain the mung beans and place them in the steamer, then set over the pan and cover with a lid. Steam for 15 minutes, or until the beans are soft. Set aside.

Meanwhile, make the pancake batter. Sift the rice flour and plain flour into a bowl, add the salt and turmeric and mix well. Pour the coconut cream and soda water into the bowl and whisk to form a smooth batter. Set aside to rest for 10 minutes.

Place a frying pan over a medium heat. Add 1 tablespoon of the oil together with the garlic and prawns and stir-fry for 2 minutes, or until the prawns are just cooked. Remove the prawns and set aside. Wipe the pan clean, then add the remaining oil and repeat this process with the pork belly.

Lightly oil a non-stick 15–18 cm (6–7 in) crêpe pan and place it over a medium heat. Sprinkle a third of the spring onion into the pan and pour a third of the batter into the centre, then pick the pan up by the handle and tip it to spread the batter over the entire surface of the pan. Pour any excess back into the original batter. (The pancake should be quite thin.)

Scatter some mung beans, school prawns, pork, spring onion and bean sprouts over half of the pancake. Season with the salt and white pepper, then reduce the heat to low and cook for about 6 minutes, or until the pancake is crisp and browned. Using a spatula, fold the pancake in half and slide it onto a large plate. Repeat with the remaining ingredients.

To serve, cut the pancakes into three or four pieces. Pick up a mustard green leaf and top it with a pancake piece and a couple of perilla and mint leaves. Roll the leaf up to form a parcel and dip it into nuoc cham before eating.

These central-style pancakes are made to order and cooked over charcoal until they're nice and crisp. They're a real textural delight – a must-try when you're in Saigon.

Central-style Pancakes
Bánh Xèo Miền Trung

< 60

**SERVES 4–6
AS PART OF A SHARED MEAL**

1 tablespoon vegetable oil
2 garlic cloves, crushed
125 ml (4 fl oz/½ cup) Tamarind Water
   (see page 152)
1 tablespoon caster (superfine) sugar
1 tablespoon fish sauce
6 duck embryo eggs, hard-boiled
   for 10 minutes
2 tablespoons crushed unsalted
   roasted peanuts
1 handful Vietnamese mint,
   torn, to serve
sea salt
freshly ground black pepper

STIR-FRIED DUCK EMBRYO EGGS WITH TAMARIND

HỘT VỊT LỘN XÀO ME

This is a little bit unusual... ok, so it's really unusual. Duck embryo egg mightn't sound too promising if you're not used to the concept but you'll see it all through Vietnam, where it's considered a delicious snack – as it is in the Philippines, Thailand and Cambodia, too. It's been eaten in these countries for centuries. The usual way to eat the egg is just boiled, peeled and with a little bit of Vietnamese mint as an accompaniment, but the place I frequent on Cô Giang does an egg embryo stir-fry, which I much prefer. The cooking process masks the look of the egg, which I'll admit can be a bit confronting. But the flavour is unlike anything else I know. For the stir-fry, the egg is first boiled and cracked, then put into a pan with tamarind, sugar and crushed peanuts and everything is cooked together, with the tamarind and other juices forming a thick sauce for the egg pieces. You have to try for yourself to know how good this tastes. If you want to cook this recipe at home, hunt down your embryo eggs at a Vietnamese greengrocer.

Heat a saucepan over a medium–high heat. Add the vegetable oil and sauté the garlic until fragrant. Add the tamarind water, sugar and fish sauce to the pan and stir to combine. When the liquid begins to bubble, crack in the duck embryo eggs and cook, stirring gently for 1 minute to coat them well with the sauce.

Season the eggs with a pinch of sea salt and black pepper, then transfer to a serving platter. Scatter over the peanuts and serve hot with Vietnamese mint.

VIETNAMESE SHAKING BEEF

BÒ LÚC LẮC

2 tablespoons oyster sauce
1 tablespoon sesame oil
1 teaspoon sugar
500 g (1 lb 2 oz) beef sirloin,
    cut into 1.5 cm (⅝ in) cubes
1 tablespoon vegetable oil
1 garlic clove, finely diced
½ small onion, cut into
    1.5 cm (⅝ in) cubes
50 g (1¾ oz) salted butter
coriander (cilantro) sprigs, to garnish
1 x quantity Soy & Chilli Dipping Sauce
    (see page 164)
steamed jasmine rice or Vietnamese
    baguette, to serve

After one of my epic Cô Giang food crawls, I always end up where the street intersects with Đề Thám. Here, you'll find one of the busiest and biggest street food stalls in the vicinity. They've got three wok cooks, right on the street, generating lots of fire and smoke and hissing sounds; it's ultra-high energy, the place is always pumping and you cannot miss it. I either order their crisp egg noodles or this dish, called 'shaking beef' in English. It's a simple stir-fry, but the secret to its success is an extremely hot wok. Your wok needs to be so hot that when you add your cubes of beef, they immediately become engulfed in flame. Don't worry, the flames die down pretty quickly, by which time they've imparted the smoky, charred flavours (or 'breath of the wok') essential to this dish, without which it would be a bit ordinary. The best way to cook it at home is in small batches, rather than the full recipe all at once, so you don't crowd the wok. And please don't cook the beef past medium or it won't taste very good at all.

Combine the oyster sauce, sesame oil, sugar and 1 tablespoon of hot water in a mixing bowl. Add the beef and toss until well coated, then cover and leave to marinate for 10 minutes.

   Heat a large wok over a high heat until smoking hot, then add the vegetable oil. Remove the beef from the marinade, add it to the wok and stir-fry for 1 minute, until sealed and charred on all sides. (If you don't have a large wok, cook the beef in two batches – this will ensure that the heat stays at a constant high temperature so that the beef doesn't stew.)

   Add the garlic, onion and butter to the wok and stir-fry for a further 2 minutes. Season with a pinch each of sea salt and black pepper, then garnish with coriander. Serve with the soy and chilli dipping sauce and steamed jasmine rice or crisp Vietnamese baguettes.

Stir-fried Duck Embryo Eggs with Tamarind *Hột Vịt Lộn Xào Me* **64**

Vietnamese Shaking Beef *Bò Lúc Lắc* **65**

PAN-FRIED RICE CAKES WITH EGG & SPRING ONIONS

BỘT CHIÊN

60 g (2¼ oz/⅓ cup) rice flour
30 g (1 oz) wheat starch
3 tablespoons vegetable oil
1 tablespoon kecap manis
    (see glossary)
1 large egg
1 spring onion (scallion), finely sliced
sea salt
freshly ground black pepper
4 tablespoons crushed roasted
    peanuts, to serve

DIPPING SAUCE
1½ teaspoons light soy sauce
1½ teaspoons dark soy sauce
¾ teaspoon rice vinegar
1½ teaspoons sugar
1 teaspoon sriracha chilli sauce

This is the Vietnamese version of a Singaporean dish called carrot cake, which doesn't contain carrots at all. But that's another story. The Vietnamese one is made with a rice flour- and wheat starch-based batter, which is steamed then cut into pieces and pan-fried. You eat the little fried 'cakes' with a lightly sweetened soy-based chilli sauce and the whole effect is a delicious snack for any time of the day. What's great about this dish are all the various textures – it's chewy, soft and moist, plus the frying gives the exterior a crispness that's addictive. My favourite place for this is on Cô Giang Street and to find it I just look for the women, or men, with huge hotplates, frying up cubes of rice cake; you can't miss them.

Mix the dipping sauce ingredients together in a mixing bowl. Set aside.

Line a 22 x 30 x 3.5 cm (8½ x 12 x 1¼ in) baking tray with plastic wrap.

Meanwhile, combine the rice flour, wheat starch, a pinch of sea salt and 250 ml (9 fl oz/1 cup) water in a small saucepan. Place over a medium heat, stirring with a whisk to form a smooth batter. As the mixture thickens, begin stirring vigorously with a wooden spoon. When the mixture has reached a smooth, gluey consistency, remove it from the heat and transfer it to the prepared baking tray. Using a spatula, smooth the mixture out into an even layer about 1 cm (½ in) thick. Cover the tray well with plastic wrap.

Half-fill a large steamer with water and bring to a rapid boil over a high heat. Set the bowl in the steamer, then cover and steam for 15 minutes. Remove from the steamer and leave to cool.

Once cool, remove the top layer of plastic wrap from the rice cake. Turn the tray over, inverting the rice cake onto a chopping board. Tap the bottom of the tray and lift it off the rice cake. Remove the remaining plastic wrap and, using a sharp knife, cut the rice cake into 2-cm (¾-in) squares. Set aside.

Heat the vegetable oil in a large frying pan over a high heat. Add the rice cakes and cook for 3 minutes, or until golden brown and crisp underneath. Reduce the heat to medium, drizzle the cakes with kecap manis, then turn the cakes over and cook for a further 3 minutes.

Meanwhile, beat the egg together with ½ teaspoon each of salt and pepper in a bowl, then stir in the spring onion, reserving 1 tablespoon to finish the dish.

Once the cakes are browned and crisp all over, pour in the egg mixture. Leave it for about 15 seconds to set, then use a spatula to turn the cakes and coat them in the egg. Add the remaining spring onion, then transfer the coated rice cakes to a serving platter and top with the crushed peanuts. Serve hot with the dipping sauce.

STIR-FRIED CORN WITH SHALLOTS AND DRIED SHRIMP

BẮP XÀO	Cô Giang Street, District 1	VND 10,000 AUD $0.75

Vietnamese adore eating sweetcorn. In Saigon, my Auntie Eight deals in wholesale corn and she brings me cobs and cobs of it, all the time. Hers is unbelievably fresh, which is how the Vietnamese like their produce, and tastes so good, no matter how I end up cooking it. I like it simply steamed or boiled, but I also enjoy it in sweet puddings too. There's a whole repertoire of sweet drink–desserts called 'che' in Vietnam that are based on coconut cream; it's really common to find bits of corn, red beans, taro, black-eyed peas and other stuff you'd not generally associate with 'pudding' in them. This quick stir-fry is a simple, tasty street snack that people go absolutely nuts over, especially young students.

VIETNAMESE COFFEE WITH CONDENSED MILK

CÀ PHÊ SỮA ĐÁ

2 teaspoons condensed milk
2 tablespoons Vietnamese
    ground coffee
ice (optional)

Introducing coffee was one of the best things the French did for Vietnam; the country is now one of the largest coffee producers in the world. The coffee grown and consumed here is mainly robusta and it's very bold in flavour with deep, nutty, caramel and even chocolate notes. They serve it strong and it's a popular pick-me-up when energy starts flagging in the intense Saigon heat. One of the nicest ways to have it is over ice, although plenty of people like it hot too. Whichever way you drink it, it's essential to use sweetened condensed milk. One of the beautiful things about drinking coffee in Saigon is the ritual of watching it filter, through a special little drip contraption called a 'phin', which sits on top of your glass. It demands you chill out and watch life go by as the coffee takes a while to drip through; you just can't be in a hurry when you order Vietnamese coffee.

Pour the condensed milk into a clear glass. Place a Vietnamese coffee drip filter on top of the glass, then remove the lid and middle screen.

Spoon the Vietnamese coffee into the filter, then tamp the ground coffee with the middle screen. Do not remove the screen.

Pour 2 teaspoons of boiling water into the filter and wait 10 seconds for the water to steep into the coffee. Now add a further 2 tablespoons of boiled water, close the lid and wait until all the water has dripped through the coffee and onto the condensed milk.

Remove the coffee filter, stir and drink hot. Alternatively, add ice for a Vietnamese iced coffee.

**Vietnamese
Coffee with
Condensed
Milk**

Cà Phê Sữa Dá

RICE PAPER ROLLS WITH PRAWN & PORK

GỎI CUỐN	Van Kiep Street, Phu Nhuan District	VND 2,500 AUD $0.15 (per roll)

Here's a dish I grew up with, and making and eating these rolls is still a favourite thing of mine to do. You see these all over Saigon at any time of the day and watching the women make them is really fascinating. They invariably remind me of how resourceful the Vietnamese are. We make these back in Sydney at my restaurant, Red Lantern, where the chefs have the luxury of long stainless steel benches with all the room in the world for their mise en place. On the street, the hawkers have no space and keep the many elements – different herbs, noodles, rice papers, prawns (shrimp), pork, dipping sauces etc. – contained on a small tray balanced on their laps. They make the rolls on the spot, fresh to order, and so perfectly neat.

DUCK & BANANA BLOSSOM SALAD

GỎI VỊT

Van Kiep Street, Phu Nhuan District

VND 40,000 AUD $2.50

One of the truly fantastic things about Vietnamese cuisine is the salad repertoire. Other Asian cuisines have salads too but they don't come close to Vietnamese versions for fresh, healthy, crunchy vibrancy, in my opinion. Salads in Saigon are really colourful, fragrant with herbs, and come with light, flavoursome, tangy dressings. If you love Vietnamese salads – and honestly, who doesn't? – and you spot a stall selling duck salad in Saigon, you must try it. The duck they use is pre-cooked, still has its skin on and is cut into pieces through the bone (it tastes better like this). Shredded banana blossom, water spinach (morning glory), sliced cabbage, Vietnamese mint, coriander (cilantro) sprigs, lightly pickled onions, crisp fried shallots, sliced carrot and radish, and peanuts are tossed together with the duck. For the dressing, they pound ginger, chilli and garlic in a mortar then add plenty of nuoc cham, with its sweet-sharp flavours of rice vinegar, fish sauce, lime and coconut juice. Textural, tasty and healthy to boot.

SEAFOOD HOTPOT

LẪU ĐỒ BIỂN

**99 Chau Van Liem Street,
Ward 14, District 5**

VND 160–280,000 AUD $10.00–17.00

The Vietnamese adore hotpot, which was most likely introduced to them, as were many other elements of Vietnamese cooking, by the Chinese. So, unsurprisingly, you find the best hotpot over in Cholon, which is Saigon's hectic Chinatown, also called District 5. The go-to place there is Dân Ích; it's the hottest hotpot joint around and gets really, really busy. Vietnamese hotpot is cooked in a round, metal trough-like vessel with a hollow chute up the middle. Cooks place the pots over really hot charcoal, pumping air though the coals to fuel the fire; flames whoosh up, out of the chute, heating the soup in the deep, circular outer part of the vessel. You then add your own choice of greens, noodles, mushrooms and other vegetables, plus whatever selection of fish and seafood you fancy. Much of this flame-fuelled cooking action happens right on the pavement and it looks super dramatic. A hot pot is a communal meal, generally an evening one, and ideally you need to eat it with at least four friends (though six or eight would be even better). Dining like this is loads of fun as you choose what you want to go into your hotpot, then dive into the bubbling stock with your chopsticks once the various bits are cooked.

SWEET SOUP

SÂM BỔ LƯỢNG

47 Tran Hung Dao B Street, District 5

VND 15,000 AUD $1.00

This hefty 'drink' may be an acquired taste for the Western palate, as its sweetness doesn't come from sugar but from all the herbs, dried fruits and seeds it contains. Vietnamese gravitate towards this when the weather is unbearably hot and humid because of the cooling effect it has on the body – not just due to the copious ice but because of all the 'cooling' properties of the medicinal ingredients ('bổ' means 'healthy'). Think of it as restoring your yin and yang. When I was a kid, this was one of the few sweet things my parents would let me have because drinking it is practically like visiting a traditional herbal doctor! Served in a glass, you can see some of the seeds, grains, leaves, fruits and other bits. There's pearl barley, dried seaweed, dried longan (a lychee-like fruit), gingko nuts, lotus seed, dried apple, just a little palm sugar and the shaved ice on top. You see it all over Saigon. Remember it when you're there and melting in the heat – I promise it will make you feel better!

**Hue Spicy
Beef & Pork
Noodle Soup**
Bún Bò Huế

84 >

SERVES 4-6

4 tablespoons shrimp paste
1 x 2 kg (4 lb 8 oz) pork leg on
    the bone, skin on, cut into
    2 equal-sized pieces
1 x 2 kg (4 lb 8 oz) gravy beef joint
    (boneless beef shin), cut into
    2 equal-sized pieces
500 ml (18 fl oz/2 cups) fish sauce
250 ml (9 fl oz/1 cup) vegetable oil
4 garlic cloves, bruised
3 white onions, sliced into rings
1 cinnamon stick, lightly pounded
4 whole cloves
2 tablespoons cracked black pepper
4 tablespoons rock salt
1 x 2 kg (4 lb 8 oz) oxtail, cut into
    3 cm (1¼ in) pieces
2 lemongrass stems,
    white part only, bruised
1 bunch spring onions (scallions),
    white stems lightly bashed, green
    parts finely sliced
1 small bunch Vietnamese mint
2 tablespoons sugar
500 g (1 lb 2 oz) thick rice vermicelli
    noodles, cooked according to
    packet instructions
1 x quantity Shrimp Paste
    & Chilli Sauce (see page 90)

TO SERVE
2 lemons, quartered
1 small bunch Vietnamese mint, torn
500 g (1 lb 2 oz) bean sprouts
bird's eye chilli, sliced
fish sauce

HUE SPICY BEEF & PORK NOODLE SOUP

BÚN BÒ HUẾ

I predict this is going to be 'the next phở'. It's a beef-based soupy noodle dish from the central Vietnamese city of Hue, the old Imperial centre, and has sour, spicy, sweet and salty notes with a predominant flavour of lemongrass. The rice noodles used are quite different to the ones used in phở; here they're thick and round and, when cooked, have a slightly resistant, al dente texture. Bún bò Huế usually features sliced, cooked beef brisket and chunks of oxtail, with cubes of pig's blood jelly starring sometimes too. There's pork hock as well, giving both flavour and plenty of lip-smacking body to the stock (the recipe here will make more of this than you need, but any excess can be stored for 3 days in the refrigerator or frozen for up to 3 months). In Saigon, when you order Bún bò Huế you always get a side basket crammed with bean sprouts, shredded banana blossom, water spinach, cabbage, sliced onions, and herbs like perilla, mint and saw-tooth coriander. You add these to the hot soup, to taste. There's also a shrimp paste and chilli dipping sauce served on the side. If you make this recipe, don't be tempted to leave it out.

Add the shrimp paste to a bowl with 500 ml (18 fl oz/2 cups) hot water. Stir to dissolve the shrimp paste and leave to steep for 1 hour, then strain and reserve the liquid, discarding the sediment.

Meanwhile, place the pork and beef in a large mixing bowl. Add 250 ml (9 fl oz/1 cup) of the fish sauce and leave to marinate for 1 hour.

Heat 2 tablespoons of the vegetable oil in a saucepan over a low–medium heat. Add the garlic and two-thirds of the onion and stir-fry until soft and translucent. Wrap the softened onions and garlic in a 30 cm (12 in) square of muslin (cheesecloth) along with the cinnamon, cloves and black pepper, and tie with kitchen string to secure. Set aside.

Add the remaining fish sauce, rock salt, oxtail and 12 litres (420 fl oz/48 cups) water to a very large saucepan or stockpot. Bring to the boil and skim off the impurities, then simmer for 30 minutes, skimming constantly.

Add the gravy beef, pork leg, lemongrass, the white part of the spring onions, the Vietnamese mint and the muslin bag to the saucepan and return to the boil, then reduce the heat and simmer for 1½ hours, skimming regularly.

Carefully remove the meat from the stock and set aside, then add the reserved shrimp paste liquid and the sugar to the pan and continue to simmer gently for a another hour, or until reduced by half. Strain the soup through a fine sieve layered with muslin and leave to cool.

To serve, pour 400 ml (14 fl oz) of stock per person into a saucepan and bring to the boil. Slice the gravy beef and pork leg into 3-mm (⅛-in) thick slices.

Divide the vermicelli noodles between individual bowls and add three beef slices, three pork slices, one oxtail piece and 2 teaspoons of the shrimp paste and chilli sauce to each. Pour over the boiling stock and top with the sliced spring onion greens and remaining onion slices.

Serve with lemon wedges, Vietnamese mint, bean sprouts and chilli slices on the side, and fish sauce and extra shrimp paste and chilli sauce for dipping.

CHARGRILLED PORK CHOPS WITH BROKEN RICE & EGG

CƠM BÌ SƯỜN

SERVES 4

4 x 200 g (7 oz) thin pork loin chops
    (about 1 cm/½ in thick)
4 large eggs
1 tablespoon vegetable oil

MARINADE

4 tablespoons oyster sauce
4 tablespoons fish sauce
1 tablespoon honey
1 tablespoon sugar
1 lemongrass stem, white part
    only, chopped
12 spring onions (scallions),
    white part only, bashed
1 garlic clove, crushed
125 ml (4 fl oz/½ cup) vegetable oil

TO SERVE

800 g (1 lb 2 oz) steamed broken rice
1 tablespoon Spring Onion Oil
    (see page 91)
1 red bird's eye chilli, sliced
1 small handful coriander
    (cilantro) leaves
2 Lebanese (short) cucumbers, sliced
2 ripe tomatoes, sliced
125 ml (4 fl oz/½ cup) Nuoc Cham
    (see page 90), for dipping

Here's another of my favourite dishes and it's one that I have for lunch two, or even three, times a week when I'm in Saigon. It not only packs a ton of flavour but has a cool backstory too. When rice is milled to separate the husks from the grains, some grains end up breaking in the process and need to be separated out from the first grade, undamaged rice. Back in the day, poor rice farmers would save this broken rice and eat it as a cheap source of food. Today, it's become something of a delicacy for the Vietnamese and is so sought after that it's actually rather expensive to buy. I love the irony of this. Why do Vietnamese people love broken rice so much? I think it's because of the texture, which is something quite special. The marinated pork in this dish requires the smokiness that comes from chargrilling to taste right, even though some vendors pan-fry it instead. So when you go to Saigon, look for ones that grill over coals. To serve, the pork goes on the rice with coriander, some cucumber, tomatoes and a bit of spring onion oil. On goes a fried egg, some lap cheong (optional; see glossary) and with tasty nuoc cham on the side, it's a perfect light meal for any time of the day.

Combine the marinade ingredients in a bowl and mix well.

Bash the pork loin chops, one at a time, with a meat mallet to a 5 mm (¼ in) thickness. Place in the marinade and turn until well coated, then cover and marinate in the refrigerator overnight.

Heat a chargrill pan or barbecue chargrill to medium–high. Chargrill the chops for 2 minutes, then turn them 90 degrees (on the same side) and cook for another 2 minutes – this should create a criss-cross pattern on the meat. Turn the chops over and repeat this process on the other side.

Meanwhile, fry your eggs. Heat the oil in a large, non-stick frying pan over a medium–low heat. Crack the eggs into the pan – if the oil starts to spit it's too hot, so turn the heat down – and cook until the tops of the whites are set but the yolks are still runny.

Remove the pan from the heat, and remove the eggs using a spatula. Place the eggs on a plate and dab with paper towels to soak up any excess oil. Set aside.

To serve, divide the broken rice and cutlets between four plates. Place a fried egg on top of each cutlet and drizzle over the spring onion oil. Garnish with the sliced chilli and coriander and accompany with the cucumber, tomato and nuoc cham.

CƠM TẤM 40A

**Chargrilled
Pork Chops
with Broken
Rice & Egg**
Cơm Bì Sườn

< 85

CRAB CLAWS WITH CHILLI SALT

CÀNG CUA RANG MUỐI ỚT	534 Vĩnh Khánh Street, District 4	VND 200,000 AUD $12.00

In Saigon, much of the interest for visitors is in District 1 and tourists inevitably end up spending a lot of time there. While it's a great place to hang out, shop and eat, if you truly want to go native, you should head to District 4. It's not far from District 1, distance-wise, but light years away in terms of how local and authentic it feels. My tip is go to 534 Vĩnh Khánh Street to a restaurant called Ốc Oanh, where you'll find some of the best seafood offerings in the entire city. They cook many delicious dishes but this crab claw one is a standout for me. To cook it they take a whole pile of crab claws, quickly steam them, then toss them in a big pot with copious amounts of dried and fresh chilli, white pepper and a ton of salt; the flavours infuse the crab. That's it. Incredibly simple and so addictively tasty. Bargain! If you go there, have the grilled scallops with spring onion (scallion) and peanuts, the chargrilled octopus and chickens' feet and the simmered snails too ('ốc' means 'snails' and they simmer them in sweet, fragrant, fresh coconut milk). The whole place is busy, fun and loud, and as you eat, busking performers come by and entertain.

NUOC CHAM

MAKES 100 ML (3½ FL OZ/½ CUP)

1½ tablespoons fish sauce
1½ tablespoons white vinegar
1 tablespoon sugar
1 garlic clove, finely chopped
½ bird's eye chilli, finely chopped
juice of ½ lime

This is one of the most used sauces in all of Vietnamese cuisine – it's served with everything from salads to bánh xèo (sizzling pancakes), to grilled meats and noodle dishes. You can tweak the balance of flavours to taste but it should always be salty from the fish sauce, a bit sour from the vinegar and lime juice, hot from the chilli and a little sweet. It's very, very simple to make.

Combine the fish sauce, white vinegar, sugar and 60 ml (2 fl oz/¼ cup) water in a saucepan over a medium heat. Stir well and cook until just before boiling point is reached, then allow to cool. Stir in the garlic, chilli and lime juice, then serve. It will keep in the refrigerator for 1 week.

SHRIMP PASTE & CHILLI SAUCE

MAKES 250 ML (9 FL OZ/1 CUP)

125 ml (4 fl oz/½ cup) vegetable oil
100 g (3½ oz) finely chopped garlic
2 lemongrass stems, white part only, finely chopped
25 g (1 oz) chilli flakes
125 ml (4 fl oz/½ cup) chilli oil
2 tablespoons mam ruoc (Vietnamese fermented shrimp paste; see glossary)

There are many types of fermented shrimp pastes produced throughout South-East Asia and for this recipe you should use the central Vietnamese one called mam ruoc. It's pinky-grey in colour and you'll find it in jars at Asian grocers. On its own it's pungent and very concentrated, but here it gives a gorgeous, deep umami flavour to the sauce. Don't be tempted to leave it out, no matter how bad you think it smells!

Place a saucepan over a medium heat, add the vegetable oil and fry the garlic until light brown. Remove the garlic from the oil and set aside. Add the lemongrass and chilli flakes to the oil and fry for 2 minutes, until lightly browned. Remove the pan from the heat and add the chilli oil to stop the cooking process. Add the fried garlic back to the oil along with the shrimp paste and mix well to combine. It will keep in the refrigerator for up to 1 month.

BASICS

SPRING ONION OIL

MAKES 250 ML (9 FL OZ/1 CUP)

250 ml (9 fl oz/1 cup) vegetable oil
6 spring onions (scallions), green part only, thinly sliced

Cooks in Vietnam use this wonderful oil as a finishing touch for all kinds of dishes; it goes particularly well with grilled meats and rice noodle dishes. It adds a lovely aroma, a touch of richness and the vibrant green colour is amazing. It's a really good way to use up green spring onion stalks that might otherwise go to waste as many recipes specify using the white part only.

Put the oil and spring onion in a saucepan over a medium heat. Cook for about 2 minutes, or until the oil just starts to simmer. Remove the pan from the heat and allow to cool.

Transfer the oil to a clean container. Do not discard the spring onion: it should be kept in the oil to garnish dishes.

It will keep in the refrigerator for several days.

FISH STOCK

MAKES 4 LITRES (140 FL OZ/16 CUPS)

2 kg (4 lb 8 oz) white fish bones (such as snapper or cod)
1 large leek, trimmed and cut into large chunks
4 cm (1½ in) piece of fresh ginger, peeled and sliced
4 garlic cloves, bruised
2 makrut (kaffir lime) leaves
1 bunch coriander (cilantro), stems and roots only

One of the quickest stocks to make, fish stock only simmers for 30 minutes – any longer and the flavour is spoiled. The usual stock-making rules apply though, i.e. don't boil it hard or it will turn cloudy. Bones from white fish give the clearest result and best flavour.

Place the fish bones in a large saucepan with 4 litres (140 fl oz/16 cups) water and bring to the boil. Skim off any impurities, then add the remaining ingredients. Return to the boil, then reduce the heat and simmer for 30 minutes. Strain through a fine sieve and allow to cool.

Store in the refrigerator for up to 3 days, or freeze until required.

INDONESIA

JAKARTA

JAKARTA

GANG GLORIA

JEMBATAN
PASAR AYAM

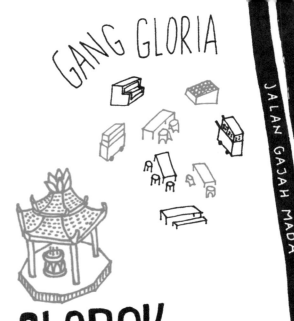

JALAN GAJAH MADA — JALAN HAYAM WURUK

JAKARTA ART
BUILDING

GLODOK
CHINATOWN

NATIONAL
MONUMENT

TANAH ABANG
MARKET

JALAN THAMRIN

PASAR
BARU

Jalan
Sabang

GITYWALK
SUDIRMAN

OLD
BATAVIA

BLOK
M

SELAMAT
DATANG
(Welcome)
MONUMENT

Capital of Indonesia and the major city of Java, the most populous island on earth, Jakarta is a vibrant, fascinating place with a unique, elegant and proud culture of its own. Yes, the streets can be off-the-charts clogged, pretty much constantly, but there's so much to see and experience (and eat!) that I'm hopeful more people will cotton on to its charms.

There's a ton of character in Jakarta. It's got an addictive, raw vitality and some mind-blowing street food, available 24/7. I love walking the busy streets and looking at all the architecture, from the shiniest of shiny shopping malls to the pockets of old, crumbling, character-filled European-style buildings – a hangover from the colonial days of the Dutch East Indies. People-wise, it's a total melting pot, with different populations from all over the far-flung archipelago living here, each bringing their dialects, their distinct ethnic character and, of course, their varied cuisines.

Tell any Jakartan that you love their food and you've got a best friend for life. Sambals, peanut sauces, great ways with offal, noodle dishes, salads, deep-fried snacks and outrageous sweets... these are just some of its key elements. There are distinctive ingredients, notably tempeh, a pressed, cake-like substance made from cultured, fermented soybeans, which they like to deep-fry. Then there are the numerous types of rice cracker that get served with practically everything. Jakartans have an addiction to crunch and deep-frying. Oh, and did I mention how much they love chilli here?

I love hanging out with passionate food blogger The Hungry Doctor; his real name is Verdi. He takes me to some places in South Jakarta that I'd never find on my own, to eat foods I'd otherwise never know about such as ketoprak, a salad that's a sister dish to gado gado. Consisting of fried tofu, sliced lontong, sprouts, vermicelli noodles and a fried egg, it's slathered in a thick, sweet, spicy peanutty sauce that's ground by hand on an enormous old stone. And the local version of cendol, a dessert–drink based on worm-like strands of green rice flour noodles, served in a glass with shaved ice, jackfruit, avocado, palm sugar, chocolate syrup and condensed milk. Believe me, when it's 37°C (98°F) and rising, this stuff is the bomb.

I hunt down the best satay in Jakarta and, here, I'm in awe of its smoky, juicy succulence. Other dishes I think I know are also a revelation. Like nasi goreng, the simple Indonesian fried rice that the whole world loves. Here, it tastes different, fresh out of the pan, rich with curry spices, white pepper and chilli paste, sweet with generous glugs of kecap manis and gamey with bite-sized bits of mutton. Oh Jakarta, you've ruined me. I have to keep coming back... and I'm bringing you with me.

AVOCADO & CHOCOLATE SMOOTHIE

JUS ALPUKAT

4 tablespoons chocolate
   sweetened condensed milk
3 ripe avocados, stones removed
4 tablespoons sweetened
   condensed milk
250 ml (9 fl oz/1 cup) full-cream
   (whole) milk
1 cup crushed ice

Having avocado in a sweet scenario might sound really unusual but being Vietnamese, I grew up with the concept and don't find it strange. We had plenty of avocado shakes and avocado ice cream as kids and I still enjoy the rich, buttery texture that avocados give to sweet snacks and desserts. On Jalan Sabang in Jakarta I do the most wonderful street food crawl – I eat satay for entrée, fried rice for my main and then I notice a tiny stand selling these shakes. I can't resist, as the Indonesian version of this long-time favourite of mine is divine. The main difference between this and a Vietnamese avocado shake is the addition of chocolate condensed milk. Yes, you heard right. Chocolate. Condensed. Milk. (On top of some regular condensed milk, I might add.) Combined with avocado and ice, it's wickedly good and you could serve this as a sweet pick-me-up or even a dessert.

Pour the chocolate sweetened condensed milk into a squeezy (chef's) bottle.

In a blender, blitz the avocado, sweetened condensed milk, full-cream milk and crushed ice together until smooth.

Squeeze the chocolate sweetened condensed milk around the inside of four tall glasses to coat. Pour the avocado smoothie into the chocolate-coated glasses and serve.

MUTTON FRIED RICE

NASI GORENG KAMBING	73 Kebon Sirih, off Jalan Sabang	IDR 15,000 AUD $1.50

Just off Jalan Sabang, down a street called Kebon Sirih, is a really famous nasi goreng joint at number 73. Theirs isn't just any nasi goreng though; they make it with mutton and the locals love it. So do I. I arrive early in the afternoon, at around 4.30 pm, because I really want to catch the cooks preparing the dish. They have two of the biggest woks I think I've seen in my life and in them they sear the mutton – kilos upon kilos of it. Next, in goes the cooked rice with all the lovely spices (curry powder, white pepper, chilli, cinnamon, cloves, curry leaves and ginger), plus heaps of sweet, sticky kecap manis (see glossary). Mutton can be a bit gamey for some as it has a particularly strong taste, but in this dish all the amazing flavours work together and the meat doesn't dominate. I love watching the way the cooks keep turning the rice in the woks; they can't stop or the mixture will burn on the base. They let me have a go and I'm tired after about a minute. This is seriously hard work – the ingredients weigh so much, they practically have to use a shovel to turn the mixture over. As they work, the air in the whole street begins to infuse with the wonderful meaty, spicy aromas and people start crowding around, waiting for it to be ready. By 6 pm, there are around 12 staff hard at work, packing nasi goreng onto plates and into folded banana leaf packets for takeaway. The pace is insane. It's maybe the busiest nasi goreng stall I've seen, which, in these parts, means it has to be one of the best. Do try and get here if you find yourself in Jakarta. It's cheap and the people are super friendly.

DUCK EGG & BEEF MARTABAK

MARTABAK SAPI	Jalan Sabang	IDR 25,000 AUD $2.50

Martabak is an Arabic word that means 'folded'. The thinking is that traders introduced this fat, stuffed flatbread from India, where it is also popular, though it originated in Yemen. There are sweet and savoury versions, although the sweet one is very different. Right on Jalan Sabang is a food truck serving martabak, it's really old and character-filled and I'm sure it's been there since way before the food truck revolution hit the world. From one side of it they serve savoury martabak and from the other they serve sweet, which I think is fantastic. You can have both in one hit! When you order a savoury one, the dough is already made, so all you need to tell them is what size you want; a regular martabak contains two duck eggs but you can have up to five! Once you order, the cook grabs a portion of dough and starts working it on her bench; it's similar to roti dough and, with a few quick slaps and turns, she's stretched it until it's super thin and translucent. It's incredible to watch, so don't blink if you find this vendor. Then she oils a sizzling hot plate and cooks the stretched dough until it blisters. Next, the filling – a mixture of the beaten duck egg, minced (ground) beef, shallots and coriander (cilantro) – gets spread over. As this cooks, and starts to firm up and resemble an omelette, the cook folds the dough over and around it to form a parcel, turning it to cook on both sides. It gets ultra crisp and golden and, when done, it's cut into pieces and served with spicy hot chilli and a sour sauce with pickled cucumber and radish. When I first tried this combination it reminded me a bit of a spring roll in concept; a crunchy wrapper, a soft, tasty interior, and a thick sauce.

SERVES 2

2 tablespoons vegetable oil

½ onion, chopped

3 garlic cloves, crushed

100 g (3½ oz) boneless, skinless
    chicken breast, thinly sliced

100 g (3½ oz) chicken gizzards,
    roughly sliced

400 g (14 oz) cooked jasmine rice

1 egg, beaten

2 cooked Indonesian beef sausages,
    roughly sliced

4 cooked Indonesian veal meatballs
    (bakso sapi), roughly chopped

45 g (1½ oz/1 cup) thinly
    sliced cabbage

45 g (1½ oz/1 cup) thinly sliced choy
    sum (Chinese flowering cabbage)

2 spring onions (scallions), sliced

1 teaspoon fish sauce

2 tablespoons kecap manis
    (see glossary)

½ tablespoon sriracha chilli sauce

1 tablespoon oyster sauce

½ teaspoon sugar

sea salt

freshly ground black pepper

2 tablespoons Fried Red Asian Shallots
    (see page 152), to garnish

CRAZY FRIED RICE

NASI GORENG GILA

**When you mention Indonesian food you automatically think of nasi
goreng, it's a dish everyone knows. But when I arrive in Jakarta, everyone
starts telling me I have to try this version. 'Gila' means 'crazy', so this
dish is literally 'crazy fried rice'. This is because they heave absolutely
everything into it; you name it, it's there. We're talking meatballs,
sausage, vegetables, chicken gizzards, shredded chicken and sometimes
even corned beef, which is a little unusual. They toss it all in a wok with
kecap manis and loads of garlic. Jalan Sabang is home to some serious
street eats and the nasi goreng gila stall, which is rather famous, is a big
reason I come down here. The cooks are so skilful with their use of the
wok. They use super large ones and I love seeing the care they take with
their rice. They cook it the day before, so it's nicely dry and doesn't clump
together; the secret of great fried rice is keeping each grain separate. The
entire time they're cooking they have their woks super hot so they impart
that distinct, smoky 'breath of the wok' into the dish. It's always packed
and lively around here, making it a great place to hang out as well as eat.**

Add half the vegetable oil to a hot wok. Add the onion and half the garlic and
sauté for 1 minute over a high heat, until fragrant. Add the chicken breast and
gizzards and stir-fry for 2 minutes, then transfer to a bowl and set aside.

Wipe the wok clean and place back over a high heat. Add the remaining oil
and garlic and the rice, and stir-fry for 3 minutes, or until the rice is slightly
browned. Push the rice to one side of the wok, then pour the beaten egg into
the empty side of the wok.

Once the egg has set, toss the rice and egg together, then add all the remaining
ingredients and season with a large pinch of salt and pepper. Toss for 2 minutes
until the rice grains are separated and slightly dry.

Transfer to individual plates and garnish with the fried shallots.

Mie Ayam is a staple noodle dish in Jakarta and can be found throughout the streets of the bustling city. This dish is full of flavour and watching it being prepared is a sight to behold, with so much action and theatre.

EGG NOODLES WITH CHICKEN & SOY

MIE AYAM

SERVES 4

2 tablespoons kecap manis
   (see glossary)
2 tablespoons worcestershire sauce
100 ml (3½ fl oz) light soy sauce
2 tablespoons vegetable oil
300 g (10½ oz) boneless,
   skinless chicken breast,
   cut into 1.5 cm (⅝ in) cubes
400 g (14 oz) fresh egg noodles
200 g (7 oz) mustard greens
   (see glossary), roughly chopped
100 g (3½ oz) bean sprouts
2 spring onions (scallions), thinly
   sliced, to garnish
2 tablespoons Fried Red Asian
   Shallots, to garnish (see page 152)

SPICE PASTE
4 garlic cloves, peeled
4 red Asian shallots, peeled
1 teaspoon ground coriander
3 cm (1¼ in) piece of turmeric,
   peeled and sliced
3 cm (1¼ in) piece of fresh ginger,
   peeled and sliced
4 candlenuts (see glossary)

CHICKEN SKIN OIL
125 ml (4 fl oz/½ cup) vegetable oil
50 g (1¾ oz) chicken skin
   (ask your local butcher),
   chopped into small pieces
2 garlic cloves, diced
1 cm (½ in) piece of fresh ginger,
   peeled and sliced
½ teaspoon ground white pepper
½ teaspoon ground coriander

This dish is incredibly popular not just in Jakarta but also throughout the country, as well as throughout the greater South-East Asian region. I find a busy stall on Jalan Sabang run by lots of men; I'm attracted by the cook preparing the fresh, yellow egg noodles and the way he's cooking them. He has a huge pot of boiling water in which he briefly blanches them and then he literally chucks them high into the air to get rid of all the water. It's very theatrical and entertaining and the whole process is over in about a minute. The hot noodles go into bowls with a bit of chicken skin oil (don't be tempted to omit it when you make this as it gives heaps of flavour and helps separate the noodles). There are lots of ingredients here but don't be put off by this, as this dish is fantastic. The addition of mustard greens and bean sprouts make it a perfect meal in a bowl.

To make the chicken skin oil, heat the vegetable oil in a small saucepan to 170°C (325°F), or until a cube of bread dropped into the oil browns in 20 seconds. Add the chicken skin to the pan and fry until crispy. Add the garlic, ginger, white pepper and ground coriander, reduce the heat to low and gently fry for 10–15 minutes, or until the garlic is lightly golden. Strain and set aside.

Combine the kecap manis, worcestershire sauce and soy sauce in a small bowl and mix together well. Set aside.

To make the spice paste, blend the garlic, shallots, coriander, turmeric, ginger and candlenuts together into a fine paste in a food processor.

Heat the vegetable oil in a wok or frying pan over a medium–high heat, add the spice paste and sauté for 2 minutes, until fragrant. Add the cubed chicken and stir-fry for 3–4 minutes, or until the chicken pieces are cooked through.

Meanwhile, bring a saucepan of water to the boil. Divide the egg noodles into four portions and blanch each separately in the boiling water for 20 seconds, then remove and refresh in iced water – this allows the noodles to develop a nice firmness. Return them to the boiling water for 10 seconds, then divide them between four serving bowls. Drizzle 1 tablespoon of chicken oil and 2 tablespoons of the kecap manis and soy sauce mixture over each noodle portion and mix well to ensure the noodles are evenly coated.

Briefly blanch the mustard greens and bean sprouts in the boiling water, then drain and divide between the four noodle bowls. Spoon over the chicken, garnish with the sliced spring onion and fried shallots and serve.

SERVES 4–6
AS PART OF A SHARED MEAL

500 g (1 lb 2 oz) boneless, skinless
   chicken thighs, cut into 4 x 5 cm
   (1½ x 2 in) pieces

MARINADE
3 garlic cloves, finely diced
2–3 red Asian shallots, thinly sliced
2 red chillies, chopped
1 teaspoon paprika
¼ teaspoon ground white pepper
2 teaspoons ground coriander
2 teaspoons ground nutmeg
1 teaspoon ground cumin
1 teaspoon vegetable oil
1 tablespoon shrimp paste
2 tablespoons light soy sauce
2 tablespoons kecap manis
   (see glossary)

SPICY PEANUT DIPPING SAUCE
1 tablespoon peanut oil
2 garlic cloves, finely diced
2 red Asian shallots, diced
4 bird's eye chillies, sliced
125 g (4½ oz) smooth peanut butter
250 ml (9 fl oz/1 cup) light
   coconut milk
3 tablespoons kecap manis
   (see glossary)
1 tablespoon worcestershire sauce
½ tablespoon light soy sauce
½ teaspoon sea salt
40 g (1½ oz/¼ cup) unsalted roasted
   peanuts, crushed
juice of 1 lime

CHICKEN SATAY SKEWERS WITH SPICY PEANUT SAUCE

SATE AYAM

In search of what they promise is the best satay, some locals send me down a main road. 'It's across from the Pertamina Hospital – just look for Sate Ayam Dankambing, on Jalan Kayai Maja, number 21', they tell me, making it all sound so easy. It isn't. I have no idea what I am looking for, only that this satay is completely worth any effort. But after I've walked about 20 metres, I see the smoke, smell the aromas and know I've found my destination. I spy two long charcoal barbecues with guys madly fanning coals. They grab around 20 beautifully threaded satay sticks at a time, submerge them in a dark, sticky marinade, and then put them straight onto the grill. Coals hiss, flames ignite, smoke puffs and the meat quickly cooks to succulent, charred perfection. The sticks are plated with sticky rice cakes, kecap manis, crispy fried shallots and a gorgeous peanut sauce. Customers eat right outside, among the smoke and fumes, sitting on wooden benches and watching the world pass by. I buy a serve of the dainty skewers; they're not huge. I get a mix of chicken and mutton, their specialities.

Soak 20 bamboo skewers in cold water for 30 minutes.

Heat a wok or saucepan over a medium heat. Add the marinade ingredients, bring to a simmer and cook for 15 minutes, or until thickened and reduced. Transfer to a large mixing bowl and leave to cool.

Thread 4–5 pieces of the chicken onto each skewer and place on a deep plate.

Repeat with the remaining chicken and skewers, then pour the marinade over the threaded chicken part of the skewers only. Cover with plastic wrap, transfer to the refrigerator and leave to marinate for 20 minutes.

To make the spicy peanut dipping sauce, heat the peanut oil in a small saucepan over a medium–high heat. Add the garlic, shallot and chilli and sauté for 3 minutes. Now add the peanut butter, coconut milk, kecap manis, worcestershire sauce, soy sauce and salt. Reduce the heat and gently simmer for 10 minutes, whisking every few minutes so that the ingredients combine well. Add the crushed peanuts, lime juice and 100 ml (3½ fl oz/½ cup) water, return to a simmer and cook for a further 2 minutes, then remove from the heat and set aside to cool.

Heat a chargrill pan or barbecue chargrill to high. Chargrill the chicken skewers for 3 minutes on each side, turning them over and basting them with the reserved marinade every minute.

Transfer to a platter and serve with the spicy peanut dipping sauce.

**Chicken Satay
Skewers with
Spicy Peanut
Sauce**
Sate Ayam

< 110

MAKES 20

2 large banana leaves,
   central ribs removed
500 g (1 lb 2 oz) snapper or
   mackerel fillets, roughly sliced
2 eggs
250 ml (9 fl oz/1 cup) coconut milk
2 teaspoons rice flour
3 makrut (kaffir lime) leaves
   (finely sliced)
1 teaspoon sea salt
1 teaspoon sugar

SPICE PASTE
8 red Asian shallots, peeled
3 garlic cloves, peeled
4 fresh red chillies
4 dried red chillies
2 lemongrass stems, white part only
3 cm (1¼ in) piece of galangal,
   peeled and chopped
3 cm (1¼ in) piece of turmeric,
   peeled and chopped
1½ tablespoons shrimp paste

SPICY FISHCAKES GRILLED IN BANANA LEAVES

OTAK OTAK

This classic street snack is found all over Jakarta and is also very common in Malaysia. It's basically a kind of fishcake formed into a long, flat rectangle, wrapped in banana leaf and grilled. I come across it in Chinatown, where an elderly woman walks through the crowds, carrying a beautiful bamboo tray stacked neatly with hundreds of them. She yells 'otak otak' as she goes, to attract customers. She's got several types; one that's pretty much just plain mackerel, pale in colour and infused with the distinctive, smoky flavour of the banana leaf. Another type is golden inside and richly flavoured with aromatics like turmeric, makrut leaves and chilli. I love both styles but the recipe I've done here is for the spicy version. It's a perfect dish for a barbecue; prep lots and serve them as a snack on their own or eat them with some rice, a sambal and a few other favourite dishes.

Cut each banana leaf into ten 6 x 10 cm (2½ x 4 in) pieces and soak in hot water for 5 minutes to soften. Wipe dry and set aside.

Put the fish, eggs, coconut milk, rice flour, makrut leaves, salt and sugar in a food processor and blend to form a rough paste. Transfer to a bowl and set aside.

Add the spice paste ingredients to the same food processor and blend together well, then return the fish paste to the food processor and blend the two pastes together until well combined.

Spread 3–4 heaped tablespoons of the fishcake paste mixture in the middle of each banana leaf piece. Now fold the sides of the leaf over tightly as you would a parcel, tucking both ends underneath and securing each with a toothpick.

Repeat with the remaining fishcake paste mixture and banana leaf pieces.

Bring a half-filled large steamer, wok or saucepan to a rapid boil over a high heat and heat a barbecue chargrill or chargrill pan to medium–high. Place the parcels in your steamer basket, seam side down, and steam, covered, for 10 minutes, then transfer to the chargrill and cook for a further 5 minutes on each side (this will give the fishcakes a nice, smoky flavour).

Unwrap the leaves and serve hot.

SILKEN TOFU WITH GINGER SYRUP

TAHWA	Gang Gloria Market, Glodok, Central Jakarta	IDR 5,000 AUD $0.50

This is one of my all-time favourite Asian-style desserts. I love it because it's got a beautiful soft texture and a subtle, ginger sweetness that make it so fabulous to eat. It also has a degree of elegance. This dish is made across Asia, but I didn't realise that included Indonesia until I started seeing it in the lovely old Gang Gloria market in Jakarta's Chinatown, which makes perfect sense as it originated in China and, where you get Chinese, you get versions of their dishes. My old mate Derice, who lives in Jakarta, brings me to Gang Gloria to show me her favourite street food places. It's such a cool market, with a buzzy, yet nostalgic vibe, especially around some of the old kopi (coffee) shops. An elderly man pushes his bicycle with a big old pot strapped to the back and, by the look of that pot, I know precisely what's in it. He scoops out the lovely, wobbly, freshly made tofu from his pot, then spoons over ginger-spiked syrup. (Sometimes they make the syrup using palm sugar and infuse it with pandan leaves (see glossary) as well as ginger.) This old guy is so proud of his tofu and is anxious for me to like it. It is sensational, with a silky, melt-in-the-mouth smoothness. He waits while I finish then takes my bowl, washes it and disappears into the crowd to find other customers. This is precisely what I love about discovering street food – meeting the hardworking people who make and serve it. I haven't included a recipe for this but it's not hard. You soak soybeans overnight then grind them and strain off the liquid before using food-grade gypsum powder to solidify the soy milk. I find it a palaver to buy and need a Chinese mate to organise it for me! An easier way is to buy your soy milk ready to go, then lightly set it using agar agar. It's cheating, but the tofu will still be delicious. Either way, when the tofu is set, pour over a light, ginger-infused sugar syrup and you're good to go.

LIGHT COCONUT NOODLE SOUP WITH BEEF & OFFAL

SOTO BETAWI

Pancoran 44, Gang Gloria Market, Glodok, Central Jakarta

IDR 50,000 AUD $5.00

'Soto' just means 'soup' and there are heaps of different sotos in Jakarta. This one consists of broth, meat, vegetables and noodles and it's a defining dish of the city – 'betawi' signifies 'Jakarta' – and you'll find it everywhere, from hole-in-the-walls to fine diners. Soto betawi is subject to variation but always contains beef. Some cooks make it creamy with milk, others keep the soup clear. My favourite version is found in Gang Gloria market in Glodok. Here, they use a turmeric-scented, milky broth containing egg noodles and vermicelli, lemongrass, chunks of potato and tomato and various cuts of beef. You choose what bits of meat you want and a typical selection includes tripe, tendons, shank and lung. The broth is really, really light and aromatic thanks to all the Indonesian bay leaves, ginger, galangal and makrut (kaffir lime) in there. Definitely look for a bowl of this when you are in Jakarta.

Lontong, Tofu & Vermicelli Salad
Ketoprak

< 122

SERVES 4 AS PART OF A SHARED MEAL

50 g (1¾ oz) bean sprouts

2 litres (70 fl oz/8 cups) vegetable oil
    for deep-frying

1 handful Indonesian red prawn
    crackers (kerupuk; see glossary)

150 g (5½ oz) firm tofu, drained and
    cut into 1.5 x 3 cm (⅝ x 1¼ in)
    rectangles

2 Lontong Rice Cakes (see page 152),
    cut into 2-cm (¾-in) chunks

100 g (3½ oz) rice vermicelli
    noodles, cooked according
    to packet instructions

1 Lebanese (short) cucumber,
    peeled and cut into batons

2 tablespoons kecap manis
    (see glossary)

2 tablespoons Fried Red Asian
    Shallots (see page 152)

PEANUT SAUCE

50 g (1¾ oz) skin-on peanuts

3 garlic cloves

2 bird's eye chillies

½ tablespoon liquid palm sugar
    (see glossary) or shaved palm
    sugar (jaggery)

½ teaspoon sea salt

LONTONG, TOFU & VERMICELLI SALAD

KETOPRAK

A healthy salad, ketoprak is similar to its better-known cousin, gado gado. It originated in Jakarta and Ketoprak Ciragil, on Jalan Cikatomas 1 in Kebayoran Baru, is the place I like to eat it. It's a busy and famous outlet, which has been going since 1961, with pastel blue walls and lovely old wooden bench tops – it's got oodles of character and locals line up outside in droves for this dish. Ketoprak is made from slices of lontong (compressed rice cake), fried tofu, vermicelli noodles, boiled egg and lots of bean sprouts. The tofu is always cooked to order, so it's hot and fresh, and I am lucky enough to get into the kitchen and watch how they make the peanut sauce on a huge stone cobek, the traditional mortar, using a pestle. The sauce is similar to the dressing for gado gado but is thicker, sweet with palm sugar and spiked with plenty of garlic. The finished dish is a lively plateful, bursting with colour, flavour and texture.

Briefly blanch the bean sprouts in boiling water, drain and set aside.

In a large wok, heat the oil to a medium–high heat, around 170°C (340°F), or until a cube of bread dropped into the oil browns in 20 seconds. Flash-fry the prawn crackers in 3 batches for a few seconds, just until they fluff up. Drain well on paper towels.

To make the peanut sauce, add the peanuts to the hot oil in the wok and fry for 2–3 minutes, or until golden brown. Remove and drain on paper towels. Add the garlic and chillies and fry for 2 minutes, then remove and drain.

In the same oil, fry the tofu for 3 minutes on each side, or until lightly browned. Drain on paper towel.

Transfer the fried peanuts, garlic and chillies to a mortar together with the palm sugar and salt and pound with a pestle to form a thick paste. Slowly add 100 ml (3½ fl oz) water and mix together well. Set aside.

To serve, divide the lontong rice cake chunks between bowls and top with the tofu, bean sprouts, vermicelli noodles and cucumber. Drizzle over the kecap manis and peanut sauce, garnish with fried shallots and serve with the red prawn crackers.

CORN FRITTER & VEGETABLE SALAD WITH PEANUT SAUCE

PECEL

Kota is the name of Jakarta's old town, and it's where you really see the influence of the Dutch. I love the history around here; there are monuments and statues, old wooden framed doorways in picturesque buildings and a big town square from when the Dutch ruled Batavia, as Jakarta was once known. Around here too is some great street food and I am drawn to a cluster of women, sitting around baskets of blanched vegetables. There's a different one in each basket and they include cassava leaves, snake beans, water spinach and bean sprouts. The women serve these, mixed on a plate, with the crispiest of corn fritters and a lovely peanut sauce flavoured with tamarind, galangal, shallots, makrut, chilli and shrimp paste.

Briefly blanch the bean sprouts in boiling water, drain and set aside. Repeat with the snake beans, cassava leaves and water spinach.

In a large wok, heat the oil to a medium–high heat, around 170°C (340°F), or until a cube of bread dropped into the oil browns in 20 seconds. Flash-fry the prawn crackers in 3 batches for a few seconds, just until they fluff up. Drain well on paper towels, keeping the wok and oil in place.

For the peanut sauce, add the peanuts to the hot oil and deep-fry for 20 seconds until golden brown. Drain on paper towel and allow to cool, then transfer to a large mortar and pound with a pestle to form a coarse paste. Transfer the paste to a small bowl to cool.

While the peanuts are cooling, add the garlic, chillies and shallots to the hot oil and fry for 3 minutes. Remove with a slotted spoon and drain on paper towel, then transfer to the mortar together with the makrut leaves, salt and lesser galangal and pound to a coarse paste. Add the tamarind pulp, palm sugar and shrimp paste and pound until fine, then return the cooled peanut paste to the mortar and mix everything together well. Transfer 250 ml (9 fl oz/1 cup) of the combined paste to a bowl, pour over 500 ml (18 fl oz/2 cups) warm water and stir together to form a sauce.

To make the corn fritters, cut the corn kernels away from the cobs using a sharp knife and transfer to a large mixing bowl. Add all the remaining fritter ingredients together with 150 ml (5 fl oz) water and mix well to form a fairly thick batter.

Return the oil for deep-frying to 170°C (340°F). With oiled hands, shape the fritters into six 8 cm (3¼ in) round discs with a thickness of 2 cm (¾ in). Carefully slide the fritters into the hot oil, in batches if necessary, and fry for 5–6 minutes, or until golden brown and crisp. Remove with a slotted spoon and drain on paper towels.

To assemble the salad, slice the corn fritters into bite-sized pieces and arrange them on a serving platter. Top with the bean sprouts, snake beans, cassava leaves, water spinach and cucumber, spoon over 3–4 tablespoons of the peanut sauce and serve with red prawn crackers and the extra sauce on the side for dipping.

SERVES 4–6
AS PART OF A SHARED MEAL

200 g (7 oz) bean sprouts
200 g (7 oz) snake (yard-long) beans, cut into 2 cm (¾ in) lengths
200 g (7 oz) cassava leaves
200 g (7 oz) water spinach (morning glory), cut into 5 cm (2 in) lengths
1 litre (35 fl oz/4 cups) vegetable oil for deep-frying
1 handful Indonesian red prawn crackers (kerupuk merah; see glossary)
2 Lebanese (short) cucumbers, halved and thinly sliced

CORN FRITTERS

2 corn cobs
75 g (2¾ oz) plain (all-purpose) flour
40 g (1½ oz) rice flour
2 spring onions (scallions), thinly sliced
2 eggs
4 red Asian shallots, diced
1 long red chilli, sliced
3 garlic cloves, finely diced
½ teaspoon sea salt
pinch of freshly ground black pepper

PEANUT SAUCE

300 g (10½ oz) skin-on peanuts
2 garlic cloves
10 long red chillies
5 bird's eye chillies
3 red Asian shallots
5 makrut (kaffir lime) leaves
1 teaspoon sea salt
4 cm (1½ in) piece of galangal, peeled
2 tablespoons tamarind pulp (with the seeds; not tamarind purée)
100 g (3½ oz) liquid palm sugar (see glossary) or shaved palm sugar (jaggery)
1 teaspoon shrimp paste

SMASHED CHICKEN WITH GREEN CHILLI SAMBAL

AYAM PENYET	A tree-lined street outside the entrance to Citywalk Sudirman	IDR 20,000 AUD $2.00

Jakarta is known for its big malls and locals love hanging out in them. They have amazing food courts but I far prefer street food and often you find some wonderful offerings in the laneways and areas just around the big malls. At around 10.30 am near the tree-lined entrance to Citywalk Sudirman, a popular mall, a whole pile of street food carts are wheeled out and start setting up shop. Later, high-rise office workers pour out of their buildings for their favourite dish and the place is pumping by lunchtime. My favourite cart is the one preparing ayam penyet – I love sitting and watching the theatre and fun of it being made. A popular East Javan dish, ayam penyet ('ayam' means 'chicken') is cooked using chicken maryland pieces that are marinated in tons of spices and deep-fried until they're exceptionally crispy. While this is happening, the cook makes the sambal. This involves deep-frying a handful of green chillies until soft, then pounding them in a cobek with some salt to make a vibrant green paste. The cooked chicken goes onto the stone as well and is smashed hard with the pestle, so the meat is torn and softened and becomes easier to eat. Next, the green sambal is slathered over and the chicken is served in a paper-lined basket with coconut rice, fried tempeh, mint and raw cabbage. And even more chilli, of course.

TURTLE & FERMENTED TOFU SOUP

PIOH TAUCO TIM

Pancoran 44, Gang Gloria Market, Glodok, Central Jakarta

IDR 50,000 AUD $5.00

'Tauco' refers to a rich, dark, sweetish soup containing fermented soybeans and 'pioh' means 'turtle'. So, this is a turtle soup. (Made using farmed animals, not any endangered or wild ones, I hasten to add!) The broth is complex in flavour – and totally delicious – while the turtle, which the Chinese believe strengthens your general health, is jelly-like and chewy. It's sort of tendon-like in texture and tastes a bit like fish but also a bit like chicken; don't be afraid to try it. Finished with a spoon of fried shallots and a sprig of coriander (cilantro), this is a popular dish in Jakarta's Chinatown, where it is in hot demand for breakfast from 7 am every morning. If you rock up late, you miss out.

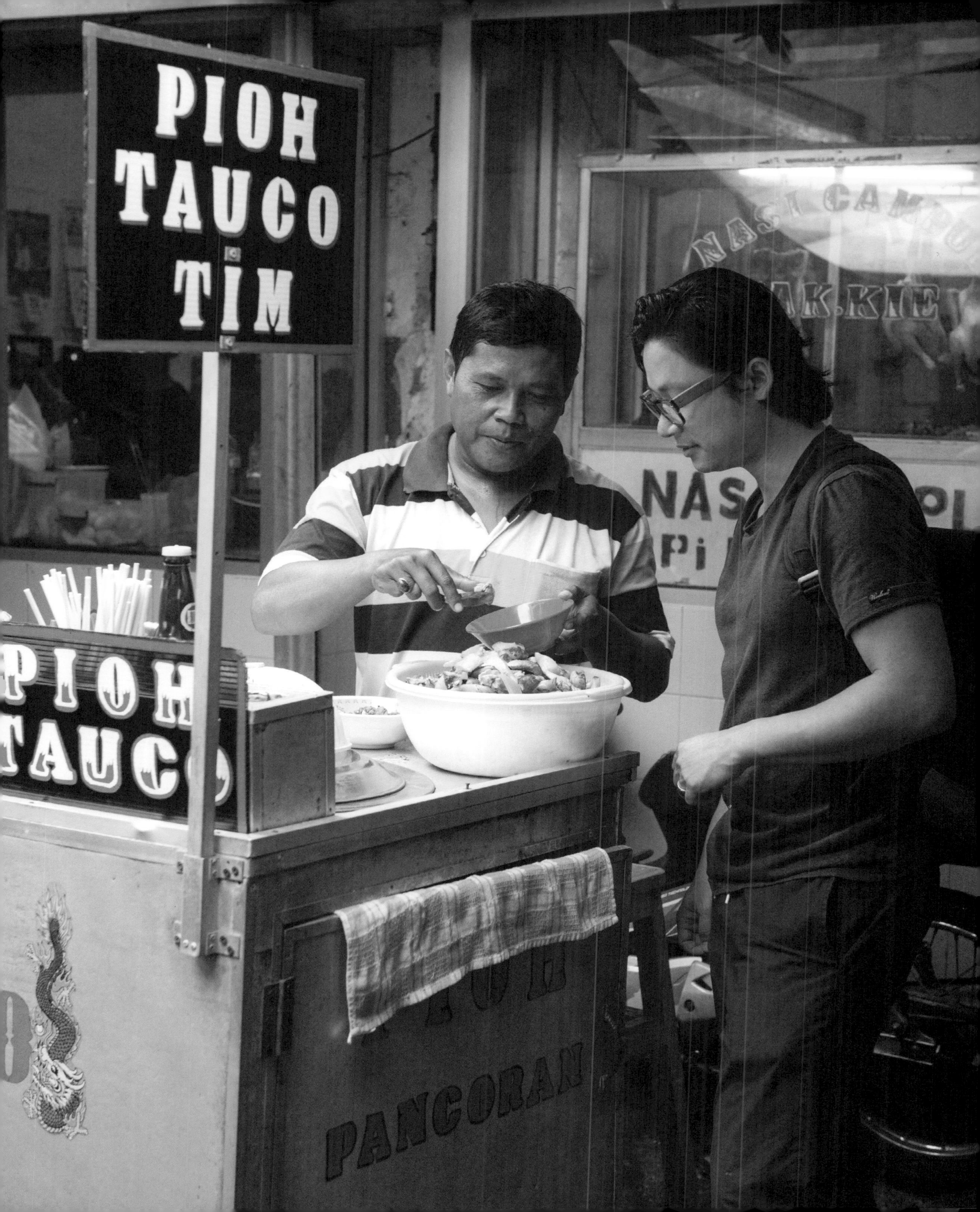
PIOH
TAUCO
TIM
PIOH
TAUCO
PANCORAN

BRAISED PORK BELLY WITH OFFAL

BEKTIM SEKBA	Pancoran 44, Gang Gloria Market, Glodok, Central Jakarta	IDR 5–15,000 AUD $0.50–1.50

Whenever I'm in Glodok, the Chinatown precinct of Jakarta, I love eating this dish because it involves pork, head to toe. Ears, tongue, belly, intestines, blood jelly; everything offaly from the pig can be found, simmering away in a massive pot on the back of a three-wheeled cart. The beautiful broth is deeply flavoured and fragrant with spices, soy sauce and kecap manis (see glossary). It's customary to eat this dish early, for breakfast. You go to the cart, point to the bits of pig you want and they serve it with boiled eggs, cucumber, tofu, fresh coriander (cilantro) and spring onion (scallion). It's a hearty breakfast that you have to try at least once! You'll find it in Gang Gloria market, along with many other really interesting – and delicious – street food options, if offal doesn't float your boat.

**Braised
Pork Belly
with Offal**
Bektim Sekba

132 >

Fish Head
Curry

SERVES 4 AS PART OF A SHARED MEAL

2 x 500 g (1 lb 2 oz) snapper heads or
    other fish heads such as salmon,
    cod or grouper
1 tablespoon sea salt
juice of 1 lime
3 tablespoons vegetable oil
2 teaspoons tamarind pulp (with the
    seeds; not tamarind purée)
3 fresh bay leaves
4 fresh curry leaves
2 lemongrass stems, white part only,
    bruised
5 cm (2 in) piece of galangal, peeled
    and diced
5 cm (2 in) piece of fresh ginger,
    peeled and diced
500 ml (18 fl oz/2 cups) coconut milk
steamed jasmine rice, to serve

SPICE PASTE

8 red Asian shallots, sliced
4 garlic cloves, sliced
5 red chillies, sliced
1 tomato, diced
3 cm (1¼ in) piece of turmeric, peeled
    and sliced
2 teaspoons ground coriander
½ teaspoon ground cumin
1 teaspoon sea salt
1 teaspoon sugar

FISH HEAD CURRY

GULAI KEPALA IKAN

As I kick around Jakarta, where I discover foods from all over Indonesia, one cuisine I really enjoy is Sundanese. It's from the western part of Java and the way they eat there is to sit down to basically a smorgasbord of pre-cooked dishes. A typical meal has a huge variety of vegetable, meat and fish options, with plenty of rice and herbs too. Little hole-in-the-walls and even street vendors specialise in this cuisine, serving so many choices it's mind-boggling. Curries, steamed dishes, deep-fried goodies; they're all here and you just pile your plate with whatever catches your fancy. It's all so appetising and the little place I really love is one that makes me feel like I'm in Morocco. Pyramids of plates piled high with food; everyone eating with their hands; an incredibly warm vibe... it honestly feels like North Africa. One of my Sundanese favourites is this fish head curry. It's not overly heavy, or terribly spicy, but it's a perfect example of the way Indonesians balance flavour so well. Oh, and don't be nervous about the idea of fish heads. There's loads of lovely meaty bits and wonderful flavour in them and sucking all of this out is a great way to eat. And then there's all that tasty, curried gravy...

Place the fish heads in a bowl with the sea salt and lime juice. Mix together well, then cover the bowl with plastic wrap and leave in the refrigerator for 30 minutes.

Meanwhile, make the spice paste. Pound all of the ingredients into a fine paste using a pestle and mortar.

Drain and discard the liquid from the fish heads. Set aside.

Heat the vegetable oil in a wok or saucepan over a low–medium heat. Add the spice paste and sauté for 5 minutes until fragrant. Add the tamarind, bay leaves, curry leaves, lemongrass, galangal and ginger and sauté for a further 2 minutes.

Add the fish heads, coconut milk and 500 ml (18 fl oz/2 cups) water to the wok, bring to a simmer and cook for 12–15 minutes, until the liquid has reduced by half and the oils are visible on the surface. Serve with steamed jasmine rice.

SWEET MARTABAK

MARTABAK MANIS

Jalan Pecenongan Raya 65A

IDR 40–140,000 AUD $4–14.00

Going to Jakarta? Then memorise this address: Jalan Pecenongan Raya 65A. Believe me, you need to go here to taste the insane, sweet martabak. I was told it was the best in the entire city and I believe it. This place is jumping all the time – people sit on tall stools in front of the stall to watch all the martabak-making theatrics and big crowds form to wait for their serve. They make the martabak in sturdy cast-iron pans, made specifically for this purpose. Essentially a fat, porous pancake or crumpet, the batter is thick and contains self-raising flour, tapioca flour, milk, sugar, eggs, yeast and baking powder. When cooked, it's deep golden on the outside but still moist and squishy in the middle and full of holes. I seriously almost have a coronary when I see what goes onto it once it's cooked. We're talking slabs of margarine, which instantly melt and get soaked up. Then loads of chopped Toblerone, sometimes Nutella, even more margarine, lots of grated cheese... you get the picture. And just when you think it can't get any more sweet or decadent, over the whole thing goes half a can of condensed milk. Chocolate martabak was the original version but now there are tons of different sorts. They make Kit Kat martabak, green tea martabak, red velvet martabak and way more. But I just go for the classic version. Once filled, it's folded over, even more margarine is spread on top and it's cut into about 10 massive pieces. I can just about manage to eat two and I have no idea how locals put away an entire serve.

FRIED TOFU WITH CHILLI & SOY

TAHU GEJROT CIREBON

SERVES 4 AS PART OF A SHARED MEAL

1 tablespoon Tamarind Water
(see page 152)
50 ml (2 fl oz) kecap manis
(see glossary)
2 tablespoons liquid palm sugar
(see glossary) or shaved
palm sugar (jaggery)
½ teaspoon sea salt
½ teaspoon rice vinegar
180 g (6 oz) fried tofu puffs,
cut into quarters

SPICE PASTE
2–6 red bird's eye chillies
(depending on how spicy you like it)
2 red Asian shallots
1 garlic clove
½ teaspoon shrimp paste

Whenever I travel, one of my joys is discovering dishes I've never tasted before. This is one. I find it by literally stumbling across a cart that's parked on the road, under a cute red umbrella. The sign mentions 'tahu' or 'tofu' and that's enough to hook me in; I love tofu. The lovely man cooking is using little mortars and pestles to make fresh batches of paste for his sauce, grinding a bit of palm sugar with some garlic, chilli, shallots and shrimp paste until smooth. He's got a batch of sauce simmering and I need to know what's in it, the aroma is so incredible. He shows me his tamarind, vinegar, kecap manis and palm sugar supplies and I work out that these are the flavours bubbling away and smelling so good. When he gets a customer he asks how many chillies they want (he gives me five!) then he grinds these up with the other paste ingredients. On go some tofu puffs and spoonfuls of the delicious sauce and that's it. I eat, standing on the street with locals, and the experience is so simple but so amazing. This, to me, is what travel is all about – meeting people and eating their favourite food with them.

To make the spice paste, pound the chillies, red shallots, garlic and shrimp paste together into a fine paste using a mortar and pestle.

Add the spice paste to a small saucepan together with the tamarind water, kecap manis, palm sugar, salt, vinegar and 200 ml (7 fl oz/¾ cup) water and bring to the boil. Reduce the heat to medium–low and simmer for 5 minutes, until just slightly reduced and the flavours have melded together.

Arrange the tofu quarters in a shallow serving bowl and pour over the sauce. Using the back of a spoon, gently press the tofu pieces down until all the sauce has been absorbed. To serve, scoop the chilli, garlic and shallot paste pieces in the sauce over the top of the tofu for colour.

**Deep-fried
Whole Fish &
Tofu with
Tomato Sambal**
Ikan Cobek

SERVES 4–6
AS PART OF A SHARED MEAL

1 tablespoon sea salt
2 tablespoons Tamarind Water
  (see page 152)
2 x 500 g (1 lb 2 oz) whole carp,
  baby barramundi or perch,
  scaled and gutted
1 litre (35 fl oz/4 cups) vegetable oil
  for deep-frying
200 g (7 oz) firm tofu, drained and
  cut into 5 x 2 cm (2 x ¾ in) squares
mint leaves, to garnish
steamed jasmine rice, to serve

TOMATO SAMBAL
4 large red chillies
2 red bird's eye chillies
1 teaspoon shrimp paste
½ teaspoon sea salt
½ teaspoon liquid palm sugar
  (see glossary) or shaved
  palm sugar (jaggery)
½ candlenut (see glossary)
1 tomato, thinly sliced

DEEP-FRIED
WHOLE FISH & TOFU
WITH TOMATO SAMBAL

IKAN COBEK

One thing I really enjoy about being in Jakarta is the sheer variety of sambals and watching people use the traditional stone mortars, or cobek, to make them by hand, and to order. It's a simple skill but the cooks are fast and precise with it and they're a joy to watch. Many Indonesian dishes have a specific sambal that accompanies them and the one for this dish involves lots of red chilli, tomato, shrimp paste and a little candlenut, pounded roughly together. Apart from an initial flash-frying of the chilli, nothing is cooked – it's such a wonderful accompaniment for the fried fish, which is briefly marinated in tamarind. It's simple but so, so fresh and that's what I love about the stall where I buy this, where all the ingredients are perfect. When they have finished cooking the fish they want to smash it hard with the pestle to loosen all the flesh and soften up the bones and I always have to step in and say 'Please! Don't! Stop!' I love picking my fish flesh off bones and they're always amused I don't want them to smash it up.

Mix together the salt and tamarind water in a bowl.

Using a large sharp knife, make three long incisions in each of the fish sides. Place in a dish, cover with the tamarind water mixture and leave to marinate for 15 minutes.

In a large wok, bring the vegetable oil to 180°C (350°F), or until a cube of bread dropped into the oil browns in 15 seconds. Brush the marinade off the fish and pat them dry with paper towels, then carefully add them to the hot oil and deep-fry for 5–7 minutes, or until just cooked and crisp. Remove and drain on paper towel.

Add the tofu to the wok and deep-fry for 5 minutes, until crisp. Drain on paper towel.

To make the tomato sambal, flash-fry the chillies in the same oil for 2 minutes until soft. Drain, then add to a mortar together with the shrimp paste, salt, sugar, candlenut and tomato and pound together well with a pestle to form a rough paste.

Transfer the fried fish to a serving platter, spoon over the sambal and garnish with mint leaves. Serve with the fried tofu and steamed jasmine rice.

BEEF CURRY

KARI SAPI

1 x 500 g (1 lb 2 oz) piece of
    beef chuck or braising steak
3 tablespoons vegetable oil
3 fresh bay leaves
4 fresh curry leaves
2 lemongrass stems, bruised
    and tied in knots
3 cardamom pods
1 star anise
1 cinnamon stick
250 ml (9 fl oz/1 cup) thick
    coconut milk
steamed jasmine rice, to serve

CURRY PASTE
3 tablespoons vegetable oil
8 red Asian shallots
8 red long chillies
6 garlic cloves
4 cm (1½ in) piece of galangal,
    peeled and sliced
4 cm (1½ in) piece of turmeric,
    peeled and sliced
½ teaspoon ground white pepper
½ teaspoon ground nutmeg
½ teaspoon ground coriander
¼ teaspoon ground cumin
2 teaspoons sea salt
1 teaspoon sugar

Around Jalan Lamandau, on serene, tree-lined streets filled with stunning, million-dollar homes, are some hidden street food gems. This peaceful oasis of upmarket real estate seems an unlikely destination for curry but that's exactly what I'm on the trail of. I've been told about Pak Lasimin's kari sapi (beef curry) and the very sound of it makes me want to a grab a bike and peddle the wide and quiet streets to find it. He's known as the pioneer of this particular dish in Jakarta so locating him is, for me, like seeking the Curry Holy Grail. And then I see his stall... or rather, I see his enormous, signature clay pot, the size of a 50-litre stockpot. Inside it is a thin, almost broth-like sauce, emitting the combined smells of cumin, nutmeg, galangal, coriander, cinnamon, turmeric, cardamom and star anise. And chunks of melting beef. The flavours are rounded and gentle, softened by coconut milk, and that chunky meat, fall-apart tender. Pak Lasimin's stand occupies an intersection, and to the right and to the left of him are areas filled with plastic tables and chairs where his happy punters sit and dine. It's an incredible place in Jakarta that you need to check out when you come.

Place the beef chuck in a large saucepan together with 1 litre (35 fl oz/4 cups) water and bring to the boil, skimming off any impurities that rise to the surface. Reduce the heat and simmer for 1 hour. Drain the beef, reserving the cooking liquor, then pat dry and cut into 5 cm (2 in) cubes.

To make the curry paste, pound the ingredients together into a fine paste using a large mortar and pestle, or in a food processor.

Heat the vegetable oil in a saucepan over a medium heat. Add the bay leaves, curry leaves, lemongrass, cardamom pods, star anise and cinnamon stick and fry for 2 minutes until fragrant. Add the curry paste and stir-fry for a further 3 minutes, then pour over the reserved beef cooking liquor and bring to the boil. Add the coconut milk and the cubed beef, bring to a simmer and cook for 1 hour, until the sauce has reduced slightly but is still quite thin and runny.

Serve with steamed jasmine rice.

Wok-tossed Hakka Noodles with Chicken & Lap Cheong
Mie Goreng Hakka **148**

Indonesian Vegetable Tofu Salad *Gado Gado* **149**

SERVES 4-6
AS PART OF A SHARED MEAL

400 g (14 oz) fresh yellow
   Hakka egg noodles
2 tablespoons peanut oil
2 garlic cloves, finely diced
150 g (5½ oz) boneless,
   skinless chicken breast,
   cut into small pieces
50 g (1¾ oz) lap cheong
   (Chinese dried sausage;
   see glossary), sliced
150 g (5½ oz) choy sum
   (Chinese flowering cabbage),
   cut into 4 cm (1½ in) lengths
150 g (5½ oz) bean sprouts
1 tablespoon sambal oelek
   chilli paste (see glossary)
2 tablespoons kecap manis
   (see glossary)
pinch of sea salt
1 tablespoon Fried Red Asian Shallots
   (see page 152), to garnish
2 spring onions (scallions), sliced,
   to garnish

WOK-TOSSED HAKKA NOODLES WITH CHICKEN & LAP CHEONG

MIE GORENG HAKKA

While checking out Block M, a bar district in Jakarta, I asked the younger locals where they went for street food. I was surprised when they directed me to the very centre of Block M where there's a newish food precinct called Food Fighters. This place is a slice of modern Jakarta so it's interesting to see, on that level alone. You can get everything here from lattes to Mexican food, to charcoal bun burgers to waffles, but I was recommended the noodles at Mie Chino. A young guy runs this place and he has just four dishes on his menu. Of these I thought the stir-fried Hakka noodles with chicken and lap cheong were pretty special. They're also easy to make and I can't recommend enough that you add them to your 'I need to cook dinner in a great hurry' repertoire. They only require simple ingredients and literally 3 minutes of cooking time, and you're there. Too easy.

Bring a saucepan of water to the boil. Blanch the noodles in the water for 20 seconds, then remove and drain. Set aside.

Heat the peanut oil in a wok over a high heat. Add the garlic and sauté until fragrant, then add the chicken and lap cheong. Stir-fry for 2 minutes.

Add the blanched noodles, choy sum and bean sprouts and stir-fry for a further minute, then add the sambal oelek, kecap manis and a pinch of salt. Stir-fry for another minute.

Transfer to individual plates, garnish with fried shallots and spring onions and serve.

INDONESIAN VEGETABLE TOFU SALAD

GADO GADO

100 g (3½ oz) bean sprouts
2 snake (yard-long) beans,
    cut into 4 cm (1½ in) lengths
150 g (5½ oz) firm tofu, drained and
    cut into 5 x 2 cm (2 x ¾ in) squares
2 Lontong Rice Cakes
    (see page 152), sliced
150 g (5½ oz) rice vermicelli noodles,
    cooked according to packet
    instructions
100 g (3½ oz/½ cup) cooked
    corn kernels

PEANUT SAUCE
1 litre (35 fl oz/4 cups) vegetable oil
    for deep-frying
3 tablespoons skin-on peanuts
4 red bird's eye chillies
1 garlic clove
pinch of sea salt
½ tablespoon liquid palm sugar
    (see glossary) or shaved
    palm sugar (jaggery)

This is one of Indonesia's most famous dishes, some reckon the country's national dish. I love the version they make near Citywalk Sudirman, where a whole bunch of carts congregate from late morning onwards. Every part of the salad, including the peanut sauce, is made to order, and the taste is rich and zingy. In Indonesian, 'gado' means to 'consume without rice' but 'gado gado' means 'mix mix'. And this salad is indeed an incredible mixture of heaps of different ingredients. Snake beans, rice vermicelli noodles, rice cakes, bean sprouts, corn... everything gets stirred together and coated with the tasty peanut sauce. I love to perch on a plastic stool and watch my favourite gado gado guy make his salads on an enormous old stone cobek; it's mesmerising. Even though a huge queue invariably forms, he still makes just one serve at a time. Never in multiples. To make the sauce, he grinds palm sugar, chilli, garlic, salt and peanuts together on the stone; this might sound 'basic' but the way he does it, it looks like art. The pragmatic chef in me always thinks it'd be far quicker to pre-make it in bulk but this is the way they roll here – everything made with intricacy, care and precision. Mind blowing. Once the sauce is smooth, he cuts up the rice cake, mixes it into the sauce with all the vegetables and some tofu and vermicelli, then places the whole thing on a plate. You help yourself to enormous rice crackers from a communal box then dig in.

Briefly blanch the bean sprouts in boiling water, drain and set aside. Repeat with the snake beans.

To make the peanut sauce, heat the oil in a wok to a medium–high heat, around 170°C (340°F), or until a cube of bread dropped into the oil browns in 20 seconds. Add the peanuts to the wok and fry for 2 minutes, or until golden brown. Remove using a slotted spoon and drain on paper towel. Leave to cool.

Add the chillies, garlic, salt and palm sugar to a mortar and pound with a pestle to a fine paste. Now add the fried peanuts and pound well until the peanuts are completely ground. Add 2–3 tablespoons of water, bit by bit, mixing well to achieve a nice, smooth sauce.

Return the oil in the wok to 170°C (340°F). Gently lower the tofu pieces into the hot oil and fry for 3–4 minutes, until browned. Remove and drain on paper towels.

Add the tofu, bean sprouts and snake beans to a large mixing bowl together with the remaining salad ingredients. Pour over the peanut sauce and toss together well.

Transfer to a platter and serve.

LONTONG RICE CAKES

MAKES 6 (SERVES 4-6)

300 g (10½ oz) jasmine rice, washed and drained
2 banana leaves, soaked in warm water to soften

Lontong is a rice staple throughout Indonesia, although you also find it in Malaysia and Singapore. Steamed inside tight tubes of banana leaves, the rice compresses and cooks to a particularly dense texture – the banana leaf makes the rice fragrant, too. Lontong is always served in slices resembling round cakes and at room temperature. You find it accompanying all sorts of dishes, including classics like gado gado and satay (see pages 149 and 110) as it goes particularly well with peanut-based sauces.

Combine the washed rice with 400 ml (14 fl oz) water and cook on a medium–high heat until the rice has absorbed all the water (the rice will be only half cooked but that's what we are looking for). Remove from the heat and cool.

Cut the banana leaves into six 25 × 25 cm (10 x 10 in) squares.

Put 4 tablespoons of the half-cooked rice onto a banana leaf square, shiny side up, and roll as tightly as you can to form a small tube. Close each end and secure with a toothpick. Repeat with the remaining ingredients.

Place the banana leaf tubes in a large saucepan and cover with water. Bring to the boil, then reduce the heat to medium and simmer, covered, for 3 hours.

Remove the banana leaf tubes from the pot and leave them to cool, then transfer them to the refrigerator and leave for 30 minutes, or until firm. Serve at room temperature.

TAMARIND WATER

MAKES 375 ML (12½ FL OZ/1½ CUPS)

100 g (3½ oz) tamarind pulp (with the seeds; not tamarind purée)

While you can buy puréed tamarind, ready to go, the flavour is not that great. Better by far is to make your own and it's not hard – a block of tamarind pulp is easy to find in Asian grocers and will keep for ages in the refrigerator. Whenever you need some tamarind water just break off a piece of tamarind, soak it briefly in boiling water, work it into a paste and sieve it to get rid of seeds and tough fibres.

Soak the tamarind pulp in 400 ml (13 fl oz) boiling water. Break it up a little with a whisk, then leave until cool enough to handle. Using your hands, break the mixture up into a rough paste. Pass the mixture through a sieve; you should get about 375 ml (12½ fl oz/1½ cups) tamarind water.

FRIED RED ASIAN SHALLOTS

MAKES 200 G (7 OZ)

200 g (7 oz) red Asian shallots, finely sliced
1 litre (35 fl oz/4 cups) vegetable oil

These are a common ingredient across Asia, where they are sprinkled over salads and rice porridge, used in stuffings and as a garnish for all manner of soup, noodle and rice dishes. Cook these in small batches for the best results and don't throw out the oil. It has a rich flavour and can be used in your cooking.

Wash the sliced shallots under cold water, then dry them with a cloth and set them aside on paper towels until completely dry. Heat the vegetable oil in a wok to 180°C (350°F), or until a cube of bread dropped into the oil browns in 15 seconds. Fry the shallots in small batches until they turn golden brown, then remove with a slotted spoon to a paper towel. They are best eaten freshly fried, but will keep for up to 2 days in an airtight container.

MALAYSIA

KUALA LUMPUR

Sprawling Kuala Lumpur is the centre of the Malay universe – a relentlessly modern dynamo of a metropolis. You have to look slightly harder for street food here but people still throng, as they've always done, to carts, stalls and casual eateries, in search of their favourite hawker-style dishes. From early in the morning until late at night, this city has a collective stomach that doesn't rest. It's my kind of place.

It's been said before but I'll say it too; Malay food could well be the original fusion cuisine. Just look at the influences on it: indigenous Malay, Chinese, Indian, Sri Lankan, English, Dutch and Portuguese, all combining to make one amazing hodgepodge. As I walk the tree-lined streets and explore hawker centres, I feel like I'm in Mumbai one minute and Beijing the next. I meet Chinese women queuing for pakoras, curry puffs and vadai in Brickfields, a staunchly Indian quarter. Meanwhile, in a Hokkien-dominated area, ethnic Indians slurp bak kut teh, a porky, herbal soup from the Chinese medicinal food tradition. So many different languages, aromas and cultures all mashed up together make Kuala Lumpur intriguing to me.

At Imbi Market, which is unbelievably busy even at 7 am, the atmosphere is frenetic, but everyone waits patiently for his or her breakfast to materialise. My favourite dish is popiah, made using fine, freshly cooked wrappers, the filling addictively crunchy with peanuts, fried breadcrumbs, fried shallots and turnip. A close second favourite are silky chee cheong fun, wide, slippery rice flour noodles topped with thick, spice-scented soybean sauce and a huge selection of garnishes. These dishes have layer upon layer of strong, complex flavours and so many textures. Everything is cooked with care, served with real passion and tastes so, so fresh. With every mouthful I fall more in love with Malaysian street food.

With every mouthful I also feel less able to walk – I'm so stuffed full! Slowing the pace down a bit, I have a great time meeting Grandma Lim, who's 74 and has been making pan mee, a type of rustic noodle that she rolls out with a beer bottle, for forty years. She serves it in a light, clear, anchovy-based broth with shiitake mushrooms and choy sum (Chinese flowering cabbage); those noodles taste gorgeous.

There's also a real sense of fun around eating here, which I think is very, very cool. Some dishes, and their cooks, take this to a whole new level; like the flying wantan man, who tosses his noodles two storeys up in the air, then catches them in his wok before cooking them. Eating 'sup gearbox' always cracks me up – who else but a Malaysian would think to serve an entire, gigantic beef hock in a bowl of flavoursome soup, complete with a straw poking out of the bone for sucking up the marrow? No one, that's who. So come explore this totally unique place with me and I'll show you a tasty thing or two.

BANANA LEAF RICE

NASI KANDAR	Usha's, Jalan Othman, Petaling Jaya Old Town	MYR 25.00 AUD $8.00

The thing that really blows me away about Kuala Lumpur is how various culinary strands all come together here. One of these is seen in the significant Indian influence and one dish from this tradition I have come to truly appreciate is Indian banana leaf rice. You literally eat steamed rice, plus an assortment of curries and accompaniments, off a large, fresh banana leaf. The go-to place for this is Usha's, a food stall on Jalan Othman in Petaling Jaya Old Town, not far from Kuala Lumpur's city centre. Usha is the matriarch-cook and she's been pulling in the locals for over 20 years with her tasty curries. One of the 'aunties' who work here will come and scoop rice onto your leaf then around that go pickles, pappadums, dhal, chutneys, maybe a boiled egg and then the curries. These are all pre-cooked and you choose the ones you want – Usha is famous for her goat tripe curry, dry mutton curry, chicken korma and salted fish curry. She also cooks mean fried chicken and fried fish and there are some unusual things on her menu, like the finely sliced bitter melon that is battered then deep-fried until it's really crispy. And her dried salted chillies, which are great. Everything is aromatic with spices and curry leaves and you eat using the fingers of your right hand. Done well, this is a super elegant way to eat. Done clumsily it's... well, a bit messy, but fun nonetheless (you can opt for cutlery if you really want). Eating here is a really warm experience as you feel like you are a guest in a family home, not at a food stall. When you've finished your meal you fold the banana leaf up, from the top down, to cover all the food bits; it's both a sign of respect and says that you've finished (and loved) the food.

MALAY CURRY PUFFS

KARIPAP

250 g (9 oz) plain (all-purpose) flour
2 teaspoons baking powder
½ teaspoon sea salt
60 g (2¼ oz) unsalted butter
1 litre (35 fl oz/4 cups) vegetable oil
   for deep-frying

FILLING
3 tablespoons vegetable oil
20 fresh curry leaves
3 cm (1¼ in) piece of fresh ginger,
   peeled and finely sliced
2 garlic cloves, finely chopped
1 onion, finely chopped
2 tablespoons Malaysian meat curry
   powder, dissolved in 2 tablespoons
   warm water
200 g (7 oz) minced (ground) beef
250 g (9 oz) potatoes, peeled and
   cut into 5 mm (¼ in) cubes
¾ teaspoon sea salt
½ teaspoon sugar

These yummy things are basically the meat pies of Malaysia (although there are vegetarian versions too) and they are soooo good. My good friend Thana takes me to Brickfields, one of the largest Indian areas of Kuala Lumpur, and we stop by Ammar's Indian Cake Stall, where he has been coming for Indian snacks since he was a young boy. It's a family-run stall that's quite famous in these parts and people flock for the delicious, inexpensive home-style snacks and cakes. When we arrive, they're doing a brisk trade in all sorts of fried goodies – you just grab a basket and take what you like from the huge assortment. They've got pakoras, appam, vadai and an addictive sweet called urundai, which look like dumplings and have soft, gooey centres filled with palm sugar. I love watching curry puffs being made. After rolling out and filling the pastry semi-circles, they use a special little cutter–crimper contraption to make the edges neat. When they're finished, they're all perfectly uniform. You can easily make curry puffs at home without one of these gizmos, the old-fashioned way, by crimping them using your fingers.

To make the filling, heat the vegetable oil in a wok, add the curry leaves, ginger, garlic and onion and sauté over a medium heat for 3–4 minutes, or until the garlic and ginger start to turn golden brown. Pour over the curry powder solution and cook, stirring, for 3 minutes, then add the beef and stir-fry for a further 3 minutes, or until browned. Now add the cubed potatoes, salt, sugar and 125 ml (4 fl oz/½ cup) water, bring to a simmer and cook for 15 minutes, stirring occasionally, until the potatoes are tender.

Transfer the filling to a bowl and set aside to cool.

Meanwhile, add the flour, baking powder, salt and butter to a large mixing bowl and mix with your fingertips until well combined. Pour in 125 ml (4 fl oz/ ½ cup) water, a little at a time, and mix until a firm dough forms, then very lightly knead for 2 minutes. Cover with plastic wrap and transfer to the refrigerator for 30 minutes to rest.

Divide the rested dough into 14 equal portions. Roll each portion into a small ball, then roll each ball out on a floured work surface into a thin circle about 8 cm (3¼ in) in diameter.

Working with one piece at a time, pick up and gently stretch a dough circle and place 1 full tablespoon of filling in its centre. Bring the bottom of the pastry to the top to form a semi-circle and pinch the edges tightly to seal. Crimp the edges with your thumb and index finger, then repeat with the remaining ingredients.

Heat the vegetable oil in a large wok to 180°C (350°F), or until a cube of bread dropped into the oil browns in 15 seconds. Fry the curry puffs in small batches for 8 minutes until they turn golden brown, crispy and flaky. Drain on a wire rack.

Serve hot or warm as a snack.

INDIAN VEGAN VADAI

VADAI

Ammar's, Jalan Tun Sambanthan, Brickfields

MYR 0.80 AUD $0.30

When you go to Kuala Lumpur, be sure to wander around Brickfields, aka Little India. There are so many Indian eateries and shops along the main drag, Jalan Tun Sambanthan, that you honestly feel you're in Mumbai. Little snack stalls are tucked here and there and Ammar's is a wildly popular one on the main street, right beside the Hong Leong Bank, in a car park. You just have to look for their white canopy and you're there. Get closer and you'll see all the aunties and uncles who work here industriously stuffing, frying and packing their sweet and savoury fried treats; they make 18 different types and these are all cooked in a little kitchen behind the stall. So they're really, really fresh. Vadai are a doughnut-shaped fritter-style snack made from lentils or split peas and there are several different varieties. I love Ammar's masala vadai, made from soaked yellow split peas and aromatics like curry leaves, turmeric, onion, chilli, ginger and garlic. They're crunchy on the outside and really light and fluffy on the inside. A handful of these is a popular breakfast.

INDIAN ROJAK

ROJAK	Opposite Taman Bahagia LRT Station	MYR 4.00 AUD $1.50

One of the most popular Malay street foods in Kuala Lumpur is rojak, which is essentially a substantial salad. There are some very distinct varieties – the Chinese one, for example, is chunky and fruit-based, with a thick, sweet-savoury dressing. It's maybe the best-known type. Indian rojak is rather different. It's a mixture of little prawn fritters, hard-boiled egg, shredded jicama, sprouts and cucumber, all drenched in a thick, sweet peanut and chilli sauce. I found a great Mamak (Indian Muslim) truck selling it and it's become my favourite place for rojak in town. You find it by taking the LRT to Taman Bahagia then walking right over the road from the station. There, beside a large tree, is my guy named Ayub – he's been making rojak for over 25 years and he's actually helping other Indian rojak trucks get set up; he's very passionate about this dish. His rojak is special because, as well as all the usual elements, he adds a spicy squid-based sauce called sotong to his. Apart from the food, I love that there are benches and tables under the nearby trees where you can take your rojak to eat; it's very tranquil as Ayub's is the only food truck here.

SERVES 4-6
AS PART OF A SHARED MEAL

600 g (1 lb 5 oz) chicken maryland
    pieces or drumsticks, cleaned
    and patted dry
400 g (14 oz) rock salt

SPICE RUB
½ teaspoon sea salt
¼ teaspoon white pepper
½ teaspoon five-spice powder
1 teaspoon ground ginger
2 cm (¾ in) piece of fresh ginger,
    peeled and thinly sliced
2 spring onions (scallions), finely sliced

SOY & CHILLI DIPPING SAUCE
4 tablespoons light soy sauce
2 bird's eye chillies, sliced

SALT-BAKED CHICKEN IN A WOK

AYAM BAKAR GARAM

My good foodie mate Evelyn, who lives in KL, takes me out for an evening of gorging at SS2 Market in Petaling Jaya, the best night market in town. It's only open on Monday night and she reckons I'll be so full by the time we finish, she'll be rolling me home. She's not wrong because, as if SS2 isn't enough, there's a nearby food street called Wai Sek Kai and it's heaving as well. There are food stalls in every direction and so many different dishes it's all a bit overwhelming. Right when I think I can't possibly cram another mouthful in, we spot a wok-full of intriguing parcels that turn out to be this dish. The chicken smells so good we can't resist. Sealed in baking paper (with seasonings Evelyn tells me are strictly Top Secret), then baked in layers of salt inside big, covered woks, it's similar in principal to the classic clay-baked beggar's chicken. Except much simpler to make. The salt keeps all the moisture in the meat and accentuates the flavours brilliantly. This is an easy dish to recreate at home and I hope you try it.

Put all the spice rub ingredients in a bowl and mix to combine. Cover the chicken pieces generously with the spice rub, then tightly wrap the pieces separately in baking paper to form parcels. Set aside.

Line the bottom of a large wok with a sheet of aluminium foil. Add half the rock salt to the wok and pour over 125 ml (4 fl oz/½ cup) water, then place the chicken parcels, fold side down, on top and cover with the remaining rock salt.

Place the wok over a high heat, cover with a lid and cook for 6 minutes, then reduce the heat to medium and cook for a further 12 minutes. Turn off the heat and leave the chicken to rest inside the wok, covered, for 30 minutes.

Meanwhile, combine the dipping sauce ingredients in a bowl and set aside.

To serve, remove the wrapped chicken from the wok, cut open the baking paper with kitchen scissors and chop each maryland into 4 pieces through the bone with a cleaver. Serve with the soy and chilli dipping sauce.

SERVES 4–6
AS PART OF A SHARED MEAL

3 lemongrass stems, white part only,
     bruised
250 ml (9 fl oz/1 cup) coconut milk
1 teaspoon sea salt
2 tablespoons liquid palm sugar
     (see glossary) or shaved
     palm sugar (jaggery)
1 tablespoon honey
1 x 1.5 kg (3 lb 5 oz) whole chicken,
     at room temperature

SPICE PASTE

6 dried chillies, seeded
6 cm (2½ in) piece of fresh ginger,
     peeled and chopped
6 cm (2½ in) piece of galangal,
     peeled and chopped
8 red Asian shallots, chopped
4 garlic cloves, chopped
4 cm (1½ in) piece of turmeric,
     peeled and chopped
1 candlenut (see glossary)
3 tablespoons Tamarind Water
     (see page 152)

TO SERVE

steamed jasmine rice
Lebanese (short) cucumber, sliced
tomatoes, sliced

ROTISSERIE CHICKEN

AYAM GOLEK

The sight of chickens cooking on a rotisserie is a common one on the busy highways of Kuala Lumpur and, as I kept seeing them, I was keen to get to the bottom of their lovely burnished colour and incredible spicy aroma. If you've ever travelled in Malaysia (or Indonesia) you'll know the locals go crazy for grilled and roasted chicken and they do it so well that it's often one of the best things you'll eat when you visit. This is a particularly popular dish to eat during Ramadan, although it's around all year long, and you'll find different versions of it in every Malaysian state. The chickens are actually cooked twice – the first time by simmering them in a sweet, spicy, coconutty braising liquid and the second by roasting. By the time they're finished, they're unbelievably juicy and succulent and infused with gorgeous flavours. You might have a rotisserie set-up at home, but if you don't, you can roast the chicken very successfully in the oven. Just remember to rest your cooked bird for 15 minutes before carving it as this allows all the juices to settle back into the meat.

To make the spice paste, pound the ingredients together into a fine paste using a large mortar and pestle, or in a food processor.

Transfer the spice paste to a wok, then add the lemongrass, coconut milk, salt, palm sugar, honey and 250 ml (9 fl oz/1 cup) water and bring to the boil.

Carefully lower the chicken, breast side first, into the wok and return to the boil, then reduce the heat to low, cover with a lid and simmer for 20 minutes.

Preheat the oven to 200°C (400°F) and line a baking tray with baking paper.

Turn the chicken over and simmer, covered, for a further 20 minutes, then remove the chicken from the sauce and place on the prepared baking tray. Roast for 25 minutes or until golden in colour.

Meanwhile, continue to simmer the sauce over a medium–high heat for 15 minutes, or until thickened and reduced by half.

Reduce the heat to 180°C (350°F). Baste the chicken generously all over with the reduced sauce, then continue to roast for a further 20 minutes until the chicken is dark golden and cooked through.

Remove from the oven and leave to rest for 15 minutes before carving. Serve with steamed rice and sliced cucumber and tomato.

FLAKY FLATBREAD & MALAYSIAN PULLED TEA WITH MILK

ROTI CANAI & TEH TARIK	Jalan 21/11b, Seapark Market, Petaling Jaya	MYR 4.00 AUD $1.50

You find roti canai at Mamak (Indian Muslim) stalls – these sell different types of roti, martabak (see pages 102 and 139) and other simple, light dishes designed to eat on the run and at any time of the day. They're everywhere in Kuala Lumpur and are kind of the Malay version of a casual burger joint. The guys that run them are consistently friendly and always have massive smiles on their faces. Two great Mamak staples are roti canai and teh tarik and I can't think of two more theatrical dishes – I never tire of watching them being made. Roti canai is a type of flatbread that is made by stretching a round of dough until it's tissue thin before being lightly smeared with ghee then expertly folded, twirled and tossed so it forms fine layers and ends up as a neat, large-ish round. Cooked on a griddle until puffy and golden, it tastes unimaginably good – especially with a mug of teh tarik, or 'pulled' tea. This speciality is made by quickly pouring milky tea between vessels from a great height to incorporate air and produce a silken texture and a foamy head. Both roti canai and teh tarik require incredible skill and they're always made to order, right in front of you, so you get to see all that fantastic action. They are absolute street food essentials when you're in Kuala Lumpur.

KAYA TOAST & HALF-BOILED EGGS

ROTI BAKAR & TELUR SEPARUH MASAK	Ah Weng Koh Hainan Tea, Imbi Market	MYR 4.00 AUD $1.50

I'm at Ah Weng Koh Hainan Tea in Imbi Market and it's just crazy. The old 'uncle' who runs the place seems a bit grouchy but maybe I would be too if I had to deal with so many orders, all at once, for drinks, toast and eggs. I learn quickly that if you don't know what you want when he comes to take your order, you're in deep trouble! He's likely to fly off at you... or simply storm away. Breakfasts are flying out of the kitchen as fast as they can make them and most people are ordering the same thing – the breakfast 'set' of kaya toast, two par-boiled eggs and Hainan tea. The deal is, you get your eggs in a big metal mug, sitting in very hot water, and leave them in there until you're ready to pull them out with the supplied tongs and crack them into a little bowl. The longer you leave them, the more they cook. Locals like theirs 'half cooked', when they're still extremely runny, and leaving them in the water for about 5 minutes accomplishes this. You crack the eggs into a bowl and mix them well with a spoon, seasoning as you go with a bit of soy sauce and pepper. This becomes the dip for your toast. At Ah Weng Koh they use soft, fluffy buns for toast (although you can also order them steamed), slathering them in home-made kaya (a jam made from coconut milk, eggs, sugar and pandan) and wedged with thick slabs of frozen butter. This combination, oozing with the runny egg dip and washed down with Hainan tea, is incredible.

COFFEE-TEA (HAINAN COFFEE)

KOPI CHAM	Ah Weng Koh Hainan Tea, Imbi Market	MYR 1.50 AUD $0.50

Although modern espresso joints are becoming more and more popular, the kopi tiam remains the bastion of the traditional local breakfast. They're fast and furious places that do a roaring trade from early in the morning and one of the best things to order is Hainan coffee. Also called 'kopi cham' ('cham' means 'to mix' in the Chinese Hokkien dialect), this tea is a mixture of seven parts milky tea to three parts coffee; it's very similar to the coffee-tea concoction called 'yuanyang' you get in Hong Kong. I am still at Ah Weng Koh Hainan Tea inside Imbi Market with my mate Chee Wah, the editor of *TimeOut Kuala Lumpur*. He invites me to meet at 6.30 am and I'm staggered by how many people are already up and about and tucking into their breakfast at this hour. Hainan coffee sounds like a weird mix but somehow it not only works, but is deliciously perfect with kaya toast and eggs, the breakfast of choice in these parts. It's smooth and velvety and exactly how they manage to get the top of it so consistently foamy every time is a closely guarded secret. You order it either hot or over ice. The origins of Hainan coffee go back to Singapore in the nineteenth century and the days of British colonialism, when Hainanese Chinese were working as domestic staff and learned Western-style cooking. During the depression of the 1930s, many of the Hainanese were forced out of domestic service and took over struggling canteens and restaurants instead. In these they served very simple food and drinks in the manner they'd learned from the British but infused with local style, including this particular coffee-tea combo. It's an interesting history and one I'd love to know more about.

I have such respect for chefs like him. He's been making Char Kuey Teow at Imbi Market for decades now, and only that dish, which he cooks to absolute perfection and with so much passion and dedication for his craft.

SMOKY FLAT NOODLES WITH PRAWNS & COCKLES

CHAR KUEY TEOW

SERVES 2

2 tablespoons vegetable oil

4 garlic cloves, diced

2 lap cheong (Chinese dried sausage; see glossary), thinly sliced on the diagonal

8 large raw tiger prawns (shrimp), peeled and deveined, leaving the tails intact

400 g (14 oz) fresh flat rice noodles, at room temperature

1 egg, briefly beaten

450 g (1 lb) cockles, cleaned and shelled

150 g (5½ oz) bean sprouts

1 bunch garlic chives, sliced into 5 cm (2 in) lengths

CHILLI PASTE

2 teaspoons vegetable oil

4 red Asian shallots, sliced

10 dried red chillies, seeded and soaked in water then sliced

2 red chillies, sliced

sea salt

SAUCE

5 tablespoons light soy sauce

1½ tablespoons dark soy sauce

1 tablespoon sugar

½ teaspoon fish sauce

½ teaspoon sea salt

large pinch of white pepper

This famous Malay dish must be cooked over extremely high heat, as getting the 'breath of the wok' into every part of it is very important. You really need to taste that smokiness and charred flavour that a super-hot wok imparts – without it it's not char kuey teow, it's just boring 'wok-fried noodles'. If you are cooking this at home on a domestic stove, which lacks the grunty heat of the burners they use on the streets of Malaysia, I suggest you cook it in two batches so you can retain as high a heat as possible. The best version of this that I know of in Kuala Lumpur is at a stall in Imbi Market. Like all other char kuey teows, it features cockles – a defining ingredient of the dish. The guy I go to sells out early (around 11 am) and once that happens, he's gone for the day. He's older, he doesn't need the money, but he cooks this dish out of pure passion. He is truly amazing.

To make the chilli paste, heat the vegetable oil in a saucepan over a medium heat, add the shallots and sauté for 1 minute. Add the dried and fresh chillies, season with salt and stir-fry for 3 minutes, until fragrant. Set aside.

Put the sauce ingredients in a bowl and mix together well.

Heat a wok a over high heat, add the vegetable oil and sauté the garlic until fragrant. Add the lap cheong and stir-fry for 1 minute, then add the prawns and stir-fry for another minute. Add the noodles to the wok and stir-fry for a further minute, or until the ingredients are slightly charred.

Push the noodle mixture to one side of the wok, then pour the beaten egg into the empty side and leave to cook for 30 seconds, or until just set. Toss the noodles and egg together, then add around 4 tablespoons of the sauce and 1–2 tablespoons of the chilli paste (depending on how spicy you want the dish to be).

Add the cockles, bean sprouts and chives and stir-fry for a final 2 minutes, then transfer to a platter or individual dishes. Serve immediately with the remaining sauce in a bowl for dipping.

VEGETARIAN FRESH SPRING ROLLS

POPIAH

1 tablespoon peanut oil
1 garlic clove, finely chopped
75 g (2¾ oz) bean sprouts
65 g (2½ oz/½ cup) grated
    daikon radish
1 small carrot, grated
50 g (1¾ oz) young fresh or tinned
    bamboo shoots, finely sliced
75 g (2¾ oz/1 cup) finely shredded
    Chinese cabbage
25 g (1 oz) glass noodles,
    soaked in hot water for
    20 minutes, then drained
60 g (2¼ oz/½ cup) finely sliced
    Asian celery (see glossary)
1 small spring onion (scallion),
    finely sliced
50 g (1¾ oz) fried tofu puffs,
    finely sliced
¼ teaspoon sea salt
¼ teaspoon sugar
1 tablespoon light soy sauce
12 butter lettuce leaves
12 popiah skins (see recipe below,
    or use frozen ones)
1½ tablespoons Fried Garlic
    (see page 214)
1½ tablespoons Fried Red Asian
    Shallots (see page 152)
1½ tablespoons chopped peanuts
Chinese-style chilli sauce, for dipping

Many Asian countries lay claim to the 'ultimate' popiah, a fresh spring roll with a really thin wrapper (made using a rather wet, wheat flour-based dough) that originated in Fujian Province in southern China. The popiah that in-the-know KL-ites flock to eat is the one at SisterS Crispy Popiah in Imbi Market – they've got a few outlets around town but this stall is the original. When you go you'll most likely see Miss Mei Lim, one of the owners, at the counter, assembling her popiah with head-spinning skill and speed. There are always long queues and every popiah is made fresh to order. They cook their own skins too (not everyone does), which makes all the difference. As the name of her stall suggests, Mei Lim loads plenty of crisp items into the filling, first spreading thick sauce over the wrapper then building up layers using bamboo shoots, fried shallots, bean sprouts, ground peanuts, grated daikon radish and more. Once the skin is stacked with filling, it's formed into a fat roll then cut into pieces. I notice people really stocking up, buying four or five popiah at a time. Do give this recipe a go – I won't pretend making popiah skins isn't an art but even if yours aren't perfect, they'll still taste better than store-bought ones.

To make the popiah skins, use an electric mixer with a paddle attachment to beat the flour, salt and 500 ml (18 fl oz/2 cups) water on a medium–high speed for 30 minutes. The dough will be ready when it is smooth, rubbery and comes away from the side of the bowl. Now knead the dough by hand, by repeatedly lifting it up and slamming it back down into the bowl until it starts to hold together in ropes. Cover and refrigerate for at least 30 minutes.

Meanwhile, heat a wok over a medium–high heat. Add the peanut oil and sauté the garlic for 1 minute, or until fragrant. Add the bean sprouts, daikon, carrot, bamboo shoots, cabbage and noodles and stir-fry for 2 minutes. Now add the celery, spring onion and tofu and stir-fry for a further minute. Season with the salt, sugar and soy sauce and stir-fry for 1 minute more. Remove the mixture from the wok and leave to cool for 5 minutes.

Divide the dough into about five small batches for easy handling. Heat a 26 cm (10½ inch) non-stick crêpe pan over a medium heat. Hold the dough with one hand and smear it over the hot pan in a circular motion, only just covering the surface of the pan. The dough should be extremely thin, and barely but evenly covering the base of the pan. Cook for 1 minute, or until the edge of the crêpe starts to curl up. Using your other hand, carefully peel the skin from the pan and place it on a plate. Continue making more skins until you have used up all the dough. (Any unused sheets can be frozen.)

To assemble the rolls, place a lettuce leaf on a popiah skin, then place a little vegetable mixture lengthways over the lettuce. Add a sprinkle of fried garlic, fried shallots and peanuts. Roll the bottom up, then fold the left and right sides in, creating an envelope. Now keep rolling up, into a nice tight roll. Repeat with the remaining ingredients.

Slice each roll into thirds and serve with chilli sauce.

POPIAH SKINS
500 g (1 lb 2 oz) plain
    (all-purpose) flour
2 teaspoons sea salt

VEGETABLES & TOFU STUFFED WITH FISH PASTE

YONG TAU FOO	Ah Fook Chee Cheong Fun, Imbi Market	MYR 2.00 AUD $0.60

I'm still at Imbi Market with my mate Chee Wah and we are eating ourselves stupid. Already I've had kaya toast, eggs and popiah and now he's suggesting we drop by Ah Fook Chee Cheong Fun, something of a mecca for Kuala Lumpur's street food devotees. The specialties here are home-made chee cheong fun (silky, slippery steamed rice noodles which you order plain or with dried shrimp; see glossary) and yong tau foo (assorted vegetables and tofu stuffed with fish paste) and, as unlikely as it may sound, you eat these together. The fish paste they use is home-made and, when cooked (by deep-frying – they deep-fry absolutely everything), it has a fantastic bouncy texture. They stuff a vast selection of vegetables including wing beans, big chillies, eggplant (aubergine), bitter melon and okra and even make little nests from snake (yard-long) beans, filling the centres of these with the paste, before you line up to choose the items you want. Everything then gets deep-fried, sliced and piled onto a plate already heaving with rice noodles. There's the option of adding fish balls, slices of Chinese doughnut and pieces of soft pig's skin and, just when you think nothing else could possibly fit onto the plate, on go lashings of thick, sweet chilli bean sauce spiked with Chinese five-spice and a scattering of white and black sesame seeds. Divine.

EGG TART

TART TELUR

Bunn Choon, Imbi Market

MYR 1.50 AUD $0.50

Another colonial legacy from the British, Hong Kong-style egg tarts are big in Kuala Lumpur. It's thought they were first baked in the 1940s by local coffee houses and over time they've become a sweet staple, with everyone having their own favourite bakery. Some use lard in their pastry (therefore they're not halal) and others butter or margarine. Some are sweeter than others and some bakers slip a bit of ginger into the silky, smooth, custardy filling. But my favourites are the ones from Bunn Choon in Imbi Market, where they've been making them since 1893, well before the invention of modern ovens, and still use their original family recipe. The tarts here are so popular they're continually baking them, so there's always a warm batch floating around – a good thing as they taste at their best when still warm. The pastry is unbelievable, it has hundreds of layers and is so crisp it practically shatters when you bite into it. Bunn Choon have also recently added an amazing-looking charcoal egg tart to their line-up – the pastry is coloured black with charcoal powder and, with their bright yellow fillings, the tarts look rather dramatic.

BLUE RICE, SHAVED COCONUT, FISH CRACKERS, CABBAGE & MORE

NASI KERABU	Bandar Baru Sungai Buloh	MYR 6.00 AUD $2.00

I find this amazing dish on a street in a quiet neighbourhood. There's a table set up on the footpath and a couple of old ladies are busy unpacking all the components for it into boxes for takeaway. Everything is really colourful but what catches my eye straight away is the rice, tinted blue using the dried petals of a type of pea flower (*Clitorea ternatea* to be botanically precise). The petals are soaked in water to extract their stunning colour and then the rice gets soaked in the blue liquid before steaming. By the time it's cooked, the rice has taken on a vivid, purplish blue – gorgeous. As well as being beautiful, the rice is also said to have medicinal benefits. It's been used for centuries in Ayurvedic treatments to enhance memory, reduce stress and for its anti-cancer properties. There's a famous cake called pulut tai tai that also uses the pea flower for colour, and you might be lucky enough to spot these in traditional kueh (cake) shops. For this dish, which originally comes from Kelantan on the east coast of Malaysia, the rice is served with assorted sides such as boiled egg, fresh coconut sambal, prawn crackers, shredded cabbage and bean sprouts. You mix it all up and eat it like a kind of rice salad. It's so fresh and light-tasting and an excellent antidote to a stinking hot Kuala Lumpur day.

**SERVES 4–6
AS PART OF A SHARED MEAL**

1 large banana leaf
1 x 800 g (1 lb 12 oz) whole
    white, firm-fleshed fish such
    as barramundi, snapper or
    leatherjacket, scaled and gutted
½ teaspoon sea salt

SPICE PASTE
4 red Asian shallots, chopped
2 garlic cloves, chopped
2 cm (¾ in) piece of fresh ginger,
    peeled and chopped
2 cm (¾ in) piece of galangal,
    peeled and chopped
2 long red chillies, sliced
1 lemongrass stem, white part
    only, chopped
2 candlenuts (see glossary)
3 makrut (kaffir lime) leaves,
    finely sliced
½ teaspoon ground turmeric
1 tablespoon fish sauce
1 tablespoon liquid palm sugar
    (see glossary) or shaved
    palm sugar (jaggery)
1 tablespoon Tamarind Water
    (see page 152)
2 tablespoons peanut oil

TAMARIND CHILLI DIPPING SAUCE
4 tablespoons Tamarind Water
    (see page 152)
½ teaspoon sea salt
½ teaspoon sugar
1 bird's eye chilli, sliced
1 red Asian shallot, sliced

TO SERVE
wing beans, sliced
Lebanese (short) cucumber, sliced
mint leaves
steamed jasmine rice

GRILLED FISH & HERBS WRAPPED IN BANANA LEAF

IKAN BAKAR

One of my favourite places to eat in Kuala Lumpur is at the huge hawker-style restaurant called Ikan Bakar Pak Lang, in Kampung Baru. It's got to be among the busiest restaurants in the entire city, with constant queues that never seem to dwindle. In the middle of the open-air dining room is a huge spread of trays filled with food that you help yourself to, buffet-style. While there are around 50 different dishes, including varieties of curries, salads, grills and fried foods, the dish I always gravitate to is their ikan bakar, or grilled fish. This is no ordinary grilled fish, however; first it's slathered in a thick paste fragrant with lemongrass, galangal, lime leaves, turmeric and chilli. Then it is wrapped in a banana leaf and cooked. As the fish grills, that fantastic paste fills the air with spicy fumes and the banana leaf scorches, giving off a lovely fragrance of its own and infusing the fish with wonderful flavours. In Malaysia they cook fish we might be unfamiliar with, but this dish translates perfectly to a backyard barbecue, using any white, firm-fleshed whole fish you prefer. They also use herbs that are only available in Asia, so I have suggested some more common herbs in this recipe.

Cut the banana leaf into a 25 x 40 cm (10 x 6 in) rectangle and soak in warm water for 5 minutes to soften. Pat dry with a clean tea towel (dish towel) and set aside.

To make the spice paste, put all the ingredients into a food processor and blitz until smooth.

Combine the tamarind chilli dipping sauce ingredients in a bowl and stir until the sugar has dissolved.

Lay the banana leaf lengthways, shiny side down, on your chopping board. Place the fish on top of the banana leaf, then score it on both sides and rub it with the sea salt. Now rub the sides and inside the cavity of the fish with the spice paste, coating it well.

Fold the leaf up, one side at a time, over the fish to form one big parcel. Pin the edges together with toothpicks to secure.

Heat a chargrill pan or barbecue chargrill to medium–high. Place the parcel on the chargrill and cook for 15 minutes on each side.

Using scissors, cut the banana leaf open and serve the fish with the tamarind chilli dipping sauce, wing beans, cucumber, mint leaves and steamed jasmine rice.

ROAST QUAIL WITH CRISP CURRY LEAVES

BURUNG PUYUH GORENG BEREMPAH

SERVES 4–6
AS PART OF A SHARED MEAL

6 x 100 g (3½ oz) quails, cleaned
500 ml (18 fl oz/2 cups) vegetable oil
50 fresh curry leaves
4 long red chillies
1 large onion, sliced
steamed jasmine rice, to serve

MARINADE
3 teaspoons five-spice powder
2 teaspoons sea salt
4 teaspoons brown sugar
2 garlic cloves, crushed
2 cm (¾ in) piece of fresh ginger,
    peeled and finely chopped
3 tablespoons light soy sauce
100 ml (3½ fl oz) vegetable oil

Another dish I enjoy at Ikan Bakar Pak Lang in Kampung Baru is roasted quails with curry leaves. The quails look (and smell) so appetising, nestled in a fluffy bed of fried onion, chillies and curry leaves. This dish is part of the restaurant's mind-boggling, help-yourself, nasi kandar selection, where you start with a big mound of steamed rice on your plate and then select curries, salads and other tantalising dishes arranged on trays to go with it. The quails are very simple to cook and they're packed with flavour, not just from the curry leaves, but from five-spice powder, fresh ginger and soy sauce too. All you need to do is marinate the quails and roast them in the oven and, while they're in there, you deep-fry the curry leaves, chillies and onions. Just don't overcook those birds – they should be slightly pink and juicy in the middle.

Put all the marinade ingredients in a large mixing bowl and mix until well combined. Add the quails, coating them well with the marinade. Cover and leave to marinate in the refrigerator for 1 hour.

Preheat the oven to 200°C (400°F).

Transfer the quails and marinade to a baking dish and roast for 15–20 minutes until the quails are lightly golden and cooked through.

Meanwhile, pour the oil into a wok and bring to 170°C (325°F), or until a cube of bread dropped into the oil browns in 20 seconds. Flash-fry the curry leaves in small batches for a few seconds, just until crisp. Remove with a slotted spoon and drain well on paper towels.

Now fry the whole chillies in the hot oil for 3 minutes, or until softened. Remove and drain. Reduce the heat to 150°C (300°F), then stir the sliced onion in the oil for 4 minutes until softened and slightly caramelised. Remove and drain.

Arrange half the crisp curry leaves and half the fried onion on a serving platter in an even layer. Top with the whole roast quails and garnish with the remaining curry leaves, onion and fried whole chillies. Serve with steamed jasmine rice.

CHICKEN RICE

NASI AYAM

Malek Tauhu, Semenyih

MYR 6.00 AUD $2.00

Malek Tauhu is a very local food stall in an area called Semenyih that's been around for thirty-something years. It was started by Malek when he retired from the police force, although these days, his daughter runs it. The place looks rather nondescript from the outside; it doesn't even have an official name, though everyone around here knows 'Malek Tauhu'. Appearances can be deceiving, however, as they attract a queue 30 deep every dinnertime. They first became famous for cucur udang, or prawn fritters, as well as their plain fried tofu, but now people flock for the chicken rice. Despite being constantly busy, I love that the atmosphere here remains quiet and calm as the family, clearly a well-oiled food-prep machine, get on with their work without talking. They all seem to intuitively know what needs to be done. Grandma chops up chicken, an 'auntie' scoops out rice while someone else is busy making a batch of their legendary chilli sauce. Both pungent and spicy, this sauce goes so beautifully with the light prawn fritters, filled with air pockets and topped with a small, fresh prawn, still in its shell. It's also the perfect foil for the chicken rice, or nasi ayam, with its melting flesh and perfectly cooked rice, each grain plump and separate. Note that nasi ayam differs from the better-known Hainanese chicken rice in that it is marinated in sweet soy sauce then roasted, giving it a gorgeously burnished, crisp skin. Hainan chicken rice is cooked by gently steeping the bird in stock, so the flesh is soft and melting and the skin pale and slippery. The roasted version puts a real Malay spin on this Chinese classic.

SWEET NOODLES WITH SHAVED ICE

CENDOL	Stall next to 7 Eleven, along Jalan Padang Belia, Brickfields	MYR 3.00 AUD $1.00

Malaysian days are extremely hot and humid and one of the things that will save you from internally frying is cendol. You see little stands all over the place, selling this popular icy sweet. Actually, you see cendol all over South-East Asia and there's a thought that the name came from the Javanese word 'jendol', which means 'swollen' or 'bump'. The theory goes that the 'bumps' in question are the pieces of green rice flour jelly that are characteristic of cendol; the traditional way to colour these is by using pandan juice. Looking a little like fat, green worms, these are a textural delight – they're a bit sticky and gelatinous and definitely chewy. Asians love them. My favourite cendol is made by a Chinese couple in Kuala Lumpur's Brickfields. On top of the all-important green 'worms', their cendol contains small cubes of grass jelly and red beans, as well as the usual shaved ice and coconut milk, sweetened with plenty of palm sugar. It's both hugely refreshing and very beautiful to look at.

FLYING WANTAN MEE WITH ROAST PORK

WANTAN MEE BABI SALAI	Jalan 22, stall next to Seapark Market, Petaling Jaya	MYR 1.50 AUD $0.50

Right next to the Seapark Market in Petaling Jaya, you'll find a guy at a stall making wantan mee. But his aren't just any old wantan mee because he makes his noodles 'fly'. Literally. After blanching the noodles for your order, he flings them really high into the air (we're talking two storeys high into the air!) deftly catches them then keeps on cooking the dish. It's so much fun to watch and whether it's just a gimmick, I'm not sure. Some people honestly reckon throwing the noodles like this makes them taste better, imparting a springier texture. I'm thinking it's a very clever way to get rid of all the water – you don't want wet noodles for this dish. Wantan mee is a street food classic in Kuala Lumpur. Basically it consists of thin egg noodles topped with an almost black sauce made from soy sauce, sesame oil and lard. Slices of sticky, sweet, home-made char siu (Cantonese barbecue pork) go over the top with some blanched choy sum (Chinese flowering cabbage). The small bowl of wantan in clear, pork-flavoured soup is to have alongside your noodles. This is considered fast comfort food in Kuala Lumpur and it's simple but delicious. Here's a tip if you want to go to the market to see my noodle hurler; he starts cooking at around 6 pm and it's best to get there early to see him in action while the light is still good.

**Flying Wantan
Mee with
Roast Pork**
*Wantan Mee
Babi Salai*

< 190

Seeing locals eating stir-fried Maggi noodles at Mamaks across Kuala Lumpur, I just had to get behind the wok and give it a go. Surprisingly, it was a really delicious dish and very simple to cook.

WOK-TOSSED INSTANT NOODLES WITH FRIED EGG

MAGGI GORENG

2 x 80 g (2¾ oz) Maggi instant noodle
  packets, plus seasoning powder
2 tablespoons vegetable oil
4 eggs
2 garlic cloves, smashed
2 bird's eye chillies, smashed
100 g (3½ oz) bean sprouts
100 g (3½ oz) choy sum
  (Chinese flowering cabbage),
  cut into 3 cm (1¼ in) lengths
85 g (3 oz) fried tofu puffs, sliced
1 tablespoon sambal oelek chilli paste
  (see glossary)
2 tablespoons oyster sauce
1 tablespoon kecap manis
  (see glossary)

After watching the flying wantan guy near Seapark Market, I find another busy stall nearby doing a roaring trade in maggi goreng. Made using good old Maggi instant noodles – in Malaysia they pronounce the hard 'g's, so it sounds like 'maggie' – this dish is actually not that unusual and you'll find it in restaurants and at Mamaks all over the place. People love it. To make it, cooks blanch and drain the instant noodles then toss them in a wok with tofu, choy sum, bean sprouts and egg. Some chilli sauce and soy sauce get thrown in, as well as the noodle seasonings from the sachet. The whole thing is served with a fried egg or two on top and it tastes great. This is the perfect dish to make when you get home late or don't have much in your cupboard.

Bring a saucepan of water to the boil. Add the noodles and blanch for 2 minutes or until al dente. Drain.

Heat a small frying pan over a medium heat. Add a tablespoon of vegetable oil, crack two of the eggs into the pan and fry, sunny side up, until the eggs are cooked but the yolks are still quite runny.

Meanwhile, bring a wok to a high heat. Add the remaining vegetable oil together with the smashed garlic and chilli and sauté for 10 seconds, then add the remaining 2 eggs and cook, stirring, until the eggs are well scrambled.

Now add the bean sprouts, choy sum, sliced tofu, noodle seasoning powder, sambal oelek, oyster sauce and kecap manis. Toss for 2 minutes.

Divide the noodle mixture between individual serving plates, top each with a fried egg and serve.

SERVES 4-6
AS PART OF A SHARED MEAL

1 x 60 g (2½ oz) bak kut teh
    spice packet
1 whole garlic bulb
1 kg (2 lb 4 oz) pork ribs,
    separated and chopped into
    6 cm (2½ in) lengths
1 tablespoon white peppercorns
2 tablespoons oyster sauce
1½ tablespoons dark soy sauce
4 tablespoons light soy sauce
1 tablespoon goji berries
sea salt
2 spring onions (scallions), sliced,
    to garnish
steamed jasmine rice, to serve
Chinese Doughnuts (see page 30),
    sliced, to serve

CHILLI, GARLIC & SOY DIPPING SAUCE

2 green bird's eye chillies, sliced
2 red bird's eye chillies, sliced
3 garlic cloves, diced
3 tablespoons kecap manis
    (see glossary)

PORK RIBS SLOW-BRAISED IN CHINESE HERBS & GOJI BERRIES

BAK KUT TEH

Klang is a small Hokkien town near Kuala Lumpur and it's home to my favourite place for eating bak kut teh – a heavily flavoured soupy stew rich with meaty, spicy and herbal elements that I just can't get enough of. Bak kut teh translates as 'meat bone tea' and a few regions claim it, each giving the dish a slightly different twist. Klang bak kut teh (and many claim Klang to be its true home) has a dark brown broth that's deeply scented, complex and intense in flavour. The one I eat at Sei Ngan Chai, a home-style restaurant with fabulously old-school decor, contains big chunks of pork still on the bone and, if you fancy them, pieces of offal and tofu puffs as well. Bak kut teh isn't difficult to make but the spices used here, which include medicinal ingredients such as angelica root, solomon's seal, Sichuan lovage and Chinese licorice as well as regular spices like cassia bark, star anise and pepper, can be tricky to find individually. To save time and hassle, just pick up a packet of the spice mix from a Chinese grocer.

Mix the dipping sauce ingredients together in a bowl. Set aside.

Rinse the dried spices, then add them to a 40 cm (16 in) square of muslin (cheesecloth), tie with kitchen string to secure and set aside.

Bring 2.5 litres (88 fl oz/10 cups) water to the boil in a large saucepan. Add the garlic and the spice bag and boil for 10 minutes, then add the pork ribs, return to the boil and cook for a further 10 minutes, skimming off any impurities that rise to the surface.

Add the white peppercorns, oyster sauce and soy sauces to the pan, reduce the heat to low and simmer gently for 50 minutes, or until the rib meat is tender and almost falling off the bone. Add the goji berries and cook for a final 10 minutes (any longer and the berries will go slightly bitter), then season with salt to taste.

Transfer to a serving platter, garnish with the spring onion and serve with the dipping sauce, steamed rice and sliced Chinese doughnuts.

**Penang
Tamarind
Fish Laksa**
Assam Laksa

200 >

SERVES 4

1 lemongrass stem, bruised

3 cm (1¼ in) piece of galangal,
    peeled and roughly sliced

1 torch ginger flower, quartered

1 x 500–600 g (1 lb 2 oz–1 lb 5 oz)
    whole mackerel, scaled and gutted

1 bunch Vietnamese mint leaves

125 ml (4 fl oz/½ cup) Tamarind Water
    (see page 152)

3 pieces of tamarind peel (optional)

2 tablespoons sugar, or to taste

4 tablespoons fish sauce, or to taste

LAKSA PASTE

1 tablespoon dried shrimp
    (see glossary), soaked in hot water
    for 15 minutes, then drained

5 dried red chillies, soaked in hot
    water for 15 minutes, then drained

7 red chillies

2 cm (¾ in) piece of galangal,
    peeled and chopped

2 cm (¾ in) piece of turmeric, peeled

1 lemongrass stem, white part
    only, chopped

5 red Asian shallots, chopped

4 garlic cloves, chopped

TO SERVE

400 g (14 oz) thick round rice
    noodles, cooked according
    to packet instructions

50 g (1¾ oz/1 cup) shredded
    iceberg lettuce

1 Lebanese (short) cucumber,
    thinly sliced into small batons

½ pineapple, sliced into small pieces

1 red onion, thinly sliced

1 torch ginger bud, finely sliced

1 bunch mint leaves

2 red bird's eye chillies, thinly sliced

1 lime, cut into wedges

1 tablespoon shrimp paste

PENANG TAMARIND FISH LAKSA

ASSAM LAKSA

For Kuala Lumpur's tastiest laksa you've got to head to Madras Lane, just off Petaling Street in the city's Chinatown. Not only will you have amazing food here but you'll also be transported back to 1960s Kuala Lumpur – it honestly looks like nothing has changed here in all that time. This place has the raw energy of a Chinese food market, with butchers hacking through bones, fish scales flying and feathers being plucked from birds by the pillowful. Right in that lane, among all the market action, you'll see a lovely couple making laksa, both assam laksa and curry laksa. While I love both types, I have a thing for the intense and unique taste of assam laksa. It's from Penang and has a sour/salty/fishy tamarind broth that contains no coconut milk at all, making it far less rich than curry laksa. The flavours are fresh and complex and some of the ingredients unusual; for example torch ginger flower and bud. You'll find it frozen in large Asian supermarkets. Assam laksa uses thick, round rice noodles which are different to the thinner, flatter variety used in curry laksa. I hope you try making this because it really is sensational.

To make the laksa paste, pound the ingredients into a fine paste using a large pestle and mortar or in a food processor.

Add 2 litres (70 fl oz/8 cups) water to a stockpot or large saucepan together with the lemongrass, galangal and torch ginger flower and bring to a rapid boil. Add the fish, reduce the heat to low and simmer for 15 minutes, skimming off any impurities that rise to the surface.

Carefully remove the fish from the broth, place in a large colander and leave to cool.

Meanwhile, strain the broth into another stockpot or large saucepan. Add the Vietnamese mint, tamarind water and tamarind peel. Bring to a simmer and cook for 10 minutes before tasting and adding the sugar and fish sauce as necessary to balance the sourness of the tamarind. Stir the laksa paste into the broth and leave to simmer for 45 minutes.

Remove the fish meat from the bones, discarding the skin and bones.

To serve, divide the noodles among four soup bowls and top with the fish meat. Add the shredded lettuce, cucumber, pineapple, red onion and fish to the bowls, then ladle over enough broth to just cover the ingredients.

Garnish with torch ginger bud, mint and chilli and serve with lime wedges and shrimp paste for an extra flavour boost.

CHICKEN & PRAWN CURRY LAKSA

MEE KARI AYAM UDANG

2 tablespoons vegetable oil
1.5 litres (53 fl oz/6 cups)
   Chicken Stock (see page 214)
500 g (1 lb 2 oz) boneless, skinless
   chicken thighs, cut into 3 cm
   (1¼ inch) chunks
1 tablespoon liquid palm sugar
   (see glossary) or shaved
   palm sugar (jaggery)
500 ml (18 fl oz/2 cups) coconut milk
500 g (1 lb 2 oz) raw tiger prawns
   (shrimp), peeled and deveined,
   leaving the tails intact
100 g (3½ oz) fried tofu puffs, halved
juice of 1 lime

LAKSA PASTE

8 dried red chillies, soaked in hot
   water for 15 minutes, then drained
2 tablespoons dried shrimp
   (see glossary), soaked in hot water
   for 15 minutes, then drained
5 red Asian shallots, chopped
4 garlic cloves, chopped
4 cm (1½ in) piece of galangal,
   peeled and chopped
2 lemongrass stems, white part only,
   finely diced
2 cm (¾ in) piece of turmeric,
   peeled and chopped
4 candlenuts (see glossary)
   or cashew nuts
1½ tablespoons mam ruoc
   (Vietnamese fermented shrimp
   paste; see glossary)
2 teaspoons ground coriander
1 teaspoon ground cumin
1 teaspoon chilli powder
3 tablespoons peanut oil

TO SERVE

400 g (14 oz) rice vermicelli noodles,
   cooked according to packet instructions
150 g (5½ oz) bean sprouts
4 coriander (cilantro) sprigs
2 tablespoons Fried Red Asian
   Shallots (see page 152)
pinch of cracked black pepper
1 lime, cut into wedges
4 tablespoons sambal oelek chilli paste
   (see glossary)

I'm not sure what it is that makes things taste amazing up here. Perhaps it's the soil and general growing conditions in Asia, or maybe it's the freshness of the coconut milk... Whatever, curry laksa in Kuala Lumpur just tastes so different to what I'm used to at home in Australia and you really have to have it here to fully experience the text-book perfect version. That's what the couple I gravitate to in Madras Lane in Chinatown make; theirs has ruined me for laksa cooked by anyone else. While there are plenty of pre-made laksa pastes on the market, I urge you not to be tempted by them and to make your own. It's not hard (we're lucky to have food processors – in the past these pastes were all made by hand), it doesn't take long at all and the difference in flavour is out of this world. You won't regret it.

To make the laksa paste, place all the ingredients except the peanut oil in a food processor. Pulse together, gradually adding the peanut oil, until a fine paste forms. Set aside.

Heat the vegetable oil in a large saucepan or stockpot over a medium heat, add the spice paste and sauté for 4 minutes until fragrant.

Now add the chicken stock and bring to the boil, then add the chicken pieces and palm sugar, reduce the heat and simmer for 5 minutes. Pour in the coconut milk and simmer for another 5 minutes, then add the prawns, tofu pieces and lime juice and cook for a further 5 minutes, until the prawns are pink and cooked through.

To serve, divide the noodles between four soup bowls and ladle over the curry broth, dividing the prawns, chicken and tofu pieces evenly. Top with the bean sprouts, coriander, fried shallots and cracked black pepper and serve with lime wedges and sambal oelek on the side.

HAND-MADE PAN MEE NOODLES WITH PORK & SHIITAKE MUSHROOMS

PAN MEE

1 tablespoon vegetable oil
2 garlic cloves, diced
3 red Asian shallots, diced
100 g (3½ oz) minced (ground) pork
8 dried shiitake mushrooms,
    soaked in hot water for
    30 minutes, then sliced
2 teaspoons oyster sauce
1 tablespoon dark soy sauce
1 tablespoon soy sauce
1½ teaspoons sugar
½ teaspoon sesame oil
1 teaspoon cornflour (cornstarch),
    mixed with 1 tablespoon water
4 litres (135 fl oz/16 cups) Pork &
    Chicken Stock (see page 292)

NOODLES
300 g (10½ oz/2 cups) plain
    (all-purpose) flour, plus extra
    for dusting
1 large egg
1 teaspoon Garlic Oil (see page 214)

TO SERVE
1 bunch choy sum
    (Chinese flowering cabbage),
    cut into 4 cm (1½ in) lengths
1 tablespoon Fried Garlic
    (see page 214)
sliced bird's eye chilli, to garnish
cracked black pepper

At Tian Yake Ban Mian in Chow Kit (at Lorong Haji Taib, Number 5, to be precise), there's a tiny old lady, now in her seventies, who's been making hand-made pan mee noodles for decades. Locals tell me her humble stall has been going since 1975. She's never missed a day of work in her life and when you see her, she's always happy. Pan mee are irregular, chopped noodles and I like taking time to watch how she makes these, completely from scratch. I love the way she rolls out her dough using a large Tiger beer bottle. She loosely folds the rolled dough up, cuts it crossways into uneven strips, then throws the fresh noodles, to order, into boiling water. She does this all day – outside and with no air-con. She is remarkable. Many noodle soup dishes like hers are all about the broth and the noodles are almost incidental. But with her pan mee, the experience is definitely all about the rustic, hand-made noodles. They go into a bowl with a subtle, light broth poured over and with tons of shiitake mushrooms and fried shallots. It's such a simple dish in many ways but there's real skill and dedication behind it. It, and the wonderful lady making her noodles with such great care, remind me again why I love street food. They're perfectly al dente and utterly delicious.

To make the noodles, combine all the ingredients together with 4 tablespoons of water in a large mixing bowl. Mix with your hands to form a dough, then knead for 5 minutes, adding a little extra water if necessary, until smooth. Cover with a damp cloth and leave to rest for 30 minutes.

Meanwhile, add the vegetable oil, garlic and shallots to a hot wok and sauté until fragrant, then add the pork and stir-fry for 3 minutes, until lightly browned. Add the mushrooms and stir-fry for a further 2 minutes, then add all the sauces, the sugar, sesame oil and 125 ml (4 fl oz/½ cup) water, reduce the heat to low and simmer gently for 6 minutes until reduced slightly. Stir in the cornflour and water mixture to thicken the mixture slightly, then transfer to a bowl and set aside.

Once the dough has rested, divide it in half. Keeping one half covered to prevent it drying out, roll out the other on a floured work surface into a 2-mm (1/16-in) thick rectangle (using a rolling pin or a large Tiger beer bottle for added authenticity). Repeat this with the other half, then slice the dough sheets lengthways into 1-cm (½-in) wide noodles. Dust your hands with flour then run your fingers through the noodles to separate them.

Briefly blanch the choy sum in boiling water, drain and set aside.

Bring the broth to the boil in a stockpot or large saucepan. Add the hand-made noodles and cook for 2–3 minutes, or until they just float to the top.

Divide the broth and noodles between four bowls, add the choy sum and pork and shiitake mix and garnish with fried garlic, sliced bird's eye chilli and cracked black pepper.

NASI LEMAK

NASI LEMAK	Jalan 21/11b, Seapark Market, Petaling Jaya	MYR 1.50 AUD $0.50

This has to be the best loved Malay dish of all time; it's considered the national dish of the country and although traditionally served for breakfast, you'll find it available at any time of the day. There are tons of variations but essential to nasi lemak is the heap of fragrant, coconut and pandan-scented rice (nasi lemak means 'coconut rice'). A large spoonful of sambal ikan bilis (a spicy, deep-flavoured sambal based around deep-fried dried anchovies) is another constant, as are toasted peanuts, a fried egg and slices or chunks of cucumber. From there, you might get a serve of curry, rendang or fried chicken on the side – there are endless possibilities, depending on the vendor. It's thought nasi lemak originated in farming areas where workers needed a substantial start to the day and it certainly delivers on that score, offering up plenty of good fats, carbs, protein and vegetables. Nowadays, you can find it pretty much everywhere – on the streets, in markets, in casual canteens and even in more expensive restaurants – sometimes wrapped up in a banana leaf, or neatly arranged on a plate. I like to order it from a Mamak stall, along with some pulled tea, and watch the world go by. Experiences don't get more 'Malay' than this.

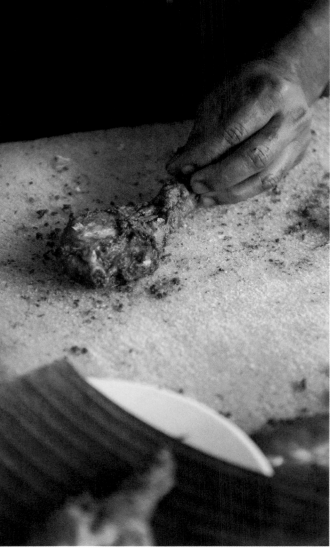

SERVES 4–6
AS PART OF A SHARED MEAL

2 tablespoons sesame oil
6 garlic cloves, peeled
8 cm (3¼ in) piece of fresh ginger,
    peeled and very finely sliced
450 g (1 lb) chicken drumsticks,
    chopped into 4 cm (1½ in)
    pieces through the bone
2 tablespoons light soy sauce
1½ tablespoons kecap manis
    (see glossary)
3 tablespoons shaoxing rice wine
    (see glossary)
1 large handful Thai basil leaves
3 spring onions (scallions), sliced into
    4 cm (1½ in) lengths, to garnish
steamed jasmine rice, to serve

THREE CUP CHICKEN

SAN BEI JI

Here's a dish that originated in south China's Jiangxi Province and one that has become incredibly popular in Malaysia. It's served as 'confinement food', fed to women in the weeks before and after they have given birth, to build up their strength and help them properly recuperate. In Malaysia, as in China, there's an entire repertoire of these confinement dishes and even today, serving them to expectant and new mothers is taken very seriously. This dish is called 'three cup chicken' because, originally, cooks used a cup each of soy sauce, rice wine and sesame oil in the dish. Traditionally it is cooked in a clay pot and this definitely adds another flavour dimension to the chicken. Even though the clay pots look rather fragile, you can actually put them over a naked flame; the trick is, you need to give them a long, overnight soaking in cold water before you first use a new one, otherwise it will most likely crack. Once soaked though, your clay pot will last for years.

Place a 4 litre (140 fl oz/16 cup) clay pot on the stove over a high heat. Add the sesame oil and whole garlic cloves and stir-fry for 30 seconds, then add the sliced ginger and sauté until fragrant.

Add the chopped chicken to the pot and stir-fry on a high heat for 2 minutes or until browned on all sides, then add the light soy sauce, kecap manis and 2 tablespoons of shaoxing rice wine and stir-fry for another 2 minutes. Cover with a lid, reduce the heat to medium–low and cook for 5–8 minutes, until the liquid has reduced to a glossy, sticky sauce and the chicken pieces are cooked through.

Return the heat to high, add the remaining 1 tablespoon of shaoxing rice wine and stir in the basil leaves. Remove from the heat.

Serve the chicken in the clay pot, garnished with the spring onion pieces and accompanied by steamed jasmine rice.

SERVES 4-6
AS PART OF A SHARED MEAL

10 chicken wings
sriracha chilli sauce, to serve

MARINADE
4 red Asian shallots, diced
4 garlic cloves, diced
6 cm (2½ in) piece of fresh ginger,
    peeled and diced
2 teaspoons sesame oil
1 teaspoon dark soy sauce
2 tablespoons light soy sauce
1 tablespoon oyster sauce
½ teaspoon sea salt
½ teaspoon ground white pepper
½ teaspoon chilli flakes
1 tablespoon honey

CHARGRILLED CHICKEN WINGS

KEPAK AYAM BAKAR

Now, I don't usually direct people to touristy areas to eat. There is, however, one strip in Kuala Lumpur where, despite being definitely touristy, I love the food – and I'm not alone in my devotion as even local food fanatics come here. The street is called Jalan Alor, it's right in the middle of the city and I head here for chicken wings. Wong Ah Wah is a massive restaurant at the end of the strip and the wings in question are their signature. There's always a queue to get in. They cook their wings on a rotisserie over charcoal, so they're charred on the outside, with juicy meat and smoky flavours inside. They go so well with a Tiger beer it's not funny. You'll come out of here smelling like barbecue but so happy you ate these wings. I promise you.

Combine the marinade ingredients in a mixing bowl and mix well. Add the chicken wings and turn to coat in the marinade, then cover with plastic wrap and marinate in the refrigerator for 1 hour.

Return the chicken wings to room temperature and heat a chargrill pan or barbecue chargrill to medium. Grill the chicken wings for 5–8 minutes on each side, turning constantly as they grill, until nicely browned all over and slightly charred.

Serve immediately with sriracha chilli sauce.

WOK-TOSSED FRAGRANT MUD CRAB

KAM HEONG CRAB

2 litres (70 fl oz/8 cups) vegetable oil
   for deep-frying
2 x 500 g (1 lb 2 oz) mud crabs,
   cleaned, claws removed and bodies
   cut into quarters
2 tablespoons dried shrimp
   (see glossary), soaked in
   hot water for 15 minutes
   and drained
3 red Asian shallots, diced
5 garlic cloves, diced
4–6 red bird's eye chillies, sliced
20 fresh curry leaves
2 tablespoons curry powder
2 teaspoons coarsely ground
   black pepper
1 tablespoon dark soy sauce
2 tablespoons oyster sauce
1 tablespoon sugar
4 coriander (cilantro) sprigs,
   to garnish

Another dish I love at Wong Ah Wah on Jalan Alor is their fragrant mud crab and you must order this as well as the wings when you visit. Whenever I dine somewhere new I always look around to see what everyone else is eating before I order and at this place, when I first tried it, just about every single customer had a plate of mud crab and chicken wings in front of them. Since then I've never ordered anything else. Their crab is a Malay take on Singapore chilli crab, with lots of intense flavours coming from curry powder, curry leaves and black pepper. The wok chefs are constantly cooking like crazy to keep up with orders, sending flames, smoke and bits of pre-cut crabs flying. The atmosphere is exciting and vibrant, with tons of kitchen noise and always so many people waiting to get a table. I notice they steam their crabs before wok-tossing them but I prefer to deep-fry mine – it's not only faster but I reckon you get a much better texture in the crab this way.

Heat the vegetable oil in a large wok or saucepan to 190°C (375°F), or until a cube of bread dropped into the oil browns in 10 seconds.

    Slide the crab claws into the wok and cook for 30 seconds, then carefully add the remaining crab pieces to the oil and deep-fry for 3–4 minutes, stirring gently as you go, until they turn deep orange in colour (depending on the size of your wok, you may need to do this in batches). Drain on paper towels.

    Transfer 2 tablespoons of the deep-frying oil to a separate wok over a high heat, then add the rehydrated shrimps and stir-fry for 1 minute. Now add the shallots, garlic, red chillies, curry leaves and curry powder and stir-fry for a further minute, or until fragrant. Add the black pepper, dark soy sauce, oyster sauce and sugar and mix together well, then return the crab pieces to the wok and toss several times to ensure they are well coated in the sauce.

    Transfer to a serving platter, garnish with the coriander and serve.

**Wok-tossed
Fragrant Mud
Crab**
*Kam Heong
Crab*

< 211

FRIED GARLIC & GARLIC OIL

**MAKES 2 TABLESPOONS FRIED GARLIC &
250 ML (9 FL OZ/1 CUP) GARLIC OIL**

250 ml (9 fl oz/1 cup) vegetable oil
6 garlic cloves, finely chopped

**Like fried red shallots, fried garlic is another
common element in South-East Asian cooking and
is used similarly. It's just as easy to make, the only
trick being not to overcook the garlic as it burns
easily. Plus, it will keep cooking in residual heat
once you remove it from the oil. The garlic-flavoured
oil that results is great for spooning over salads
and noodle dishes.**

Add the vegetable oil to a wok and heat to 180°C (350°F),
or until a cube of bread dropped into the oil browns in
15 seconds. Add the garlic cloves and fry until golden – be
careful not to overcook the garlic, as it will keep cooking
once it is removed from the heat.

Remove the garlic with a slotted spoon and drain on
paper towels.

Store the fried garlic in an airtight container for up
to 4 days. The garlic oil will keep for up to 2 weeks if stored
in a cool place.

CHICKEN STOCK

**MAKES 5 LITRES
(175 FL OZ/20 CUPS)**

6 garlic cloves
8 spring onions (scallions), white part only, roughly chopped
1 x 1.6 kg (3 lb 8 oz) whole chicken
4 cm (1½ in) piece of fresh ginger, peeled and sliced

**As the most used stock in this book, it's well worth
your while perfecting chicken stock. It needs very
little hands-on work; in fact, once you've skimmed
off all the impurities and it's settled into a nice,
gentle simmer, you can forget about it for 2 hours.
Just don't let it boil or it will evaporate too much
and may turn cloudy.**

Pound the garlic and spring onions into a paste using
a pestle and mortar or whizz together using a food
processor. Wash the chicken thoroughly under cold
running water, making sure to remove all traces of blood,
guts and fat from the cavity. Place the chicken in a large
saucepan or stockpot with 6 litres (210 fl oz/24 cups)
water and bring to the boil.

Reduce the heat of the stock to a slow simmer and skim
the surface. Continue to skim for 10 minutes until you have
removed most of the fat, then add the ginger to the pan
with the garlic and spring onion paste. Cook for a further
2 hours, then strain and allow the stock to cool. Refrigerate
for up to 3 days or freeze until required.

THAILAND

BANGKOK

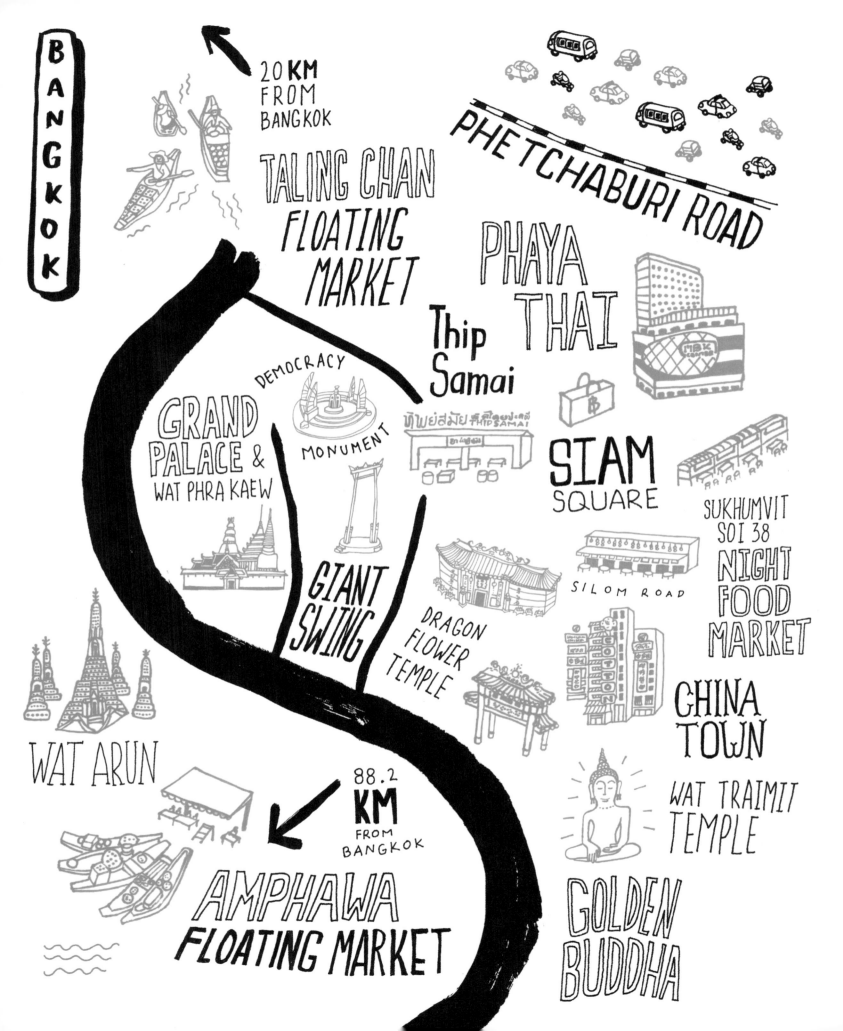

'Aroy'. It means 'delicious', it's my favourite Thai word and if two syllables could possibly sum up Bangkok's street food (which they can't), these would be them. It's been said over and over that Bangkok is one of the best places in the world for street food and I absolutely agree; this place to me is just one giant excuse to eat outdoors.

The street food repertoire here is complex. With myriad ingredients, influences, cooking techniques, flavours and textures at work, the food, like the city itself, represents sensory overload. Being the Thai capital, there's food from every Thai region available, from the fiery, pungent, sour dishes of north-eastern Isaan Province, where sticky rice is king, to the rich, complex, coconut-milk infused dishes, and curries, of the central plains and the south.

I love the fact that, without looking very hard, I can buy a salad like som tum (green papaya), muddled to order in a wooden mortar, next to a cart dispensing khanom bueang (crisp, wafer-thin coconut pancakes that are an art to make, with sweet and salty fillings) near another cooking khao kha moo, or pork hock simmered with eggs in a heady, spice-fragrant stock. There's a Chinese influence in Thai cooking that's given rise to a whole range of dishes, plus an entire precinct of town. Then there's Thai Muslim food, with distinct Indian influences. There's so much to know about food in this city and I won't be exhausting it any time soon.

Not all the food is great, though. Like many places around the world, standards are declining, with shortcuts routinely taken and pre-made pastes, and other convenience materials, in common use. So whenever I'm here, I call on expert local knowledge to point me to vendors making their dishes completely from scratch. Like the tiny place down Soi Convent off Silom Road that does haan pa low, or goose simmered with five-spice powder, a dish that's normally hard to find. Succulent, rich and deep-flavoured, it nearly knocks me off my chair every time I have it. Or Thip Samai, considered the best place on earth for pad thai, with a frantic kitchen that spills out onto the busy curb of Mahachai Road. Diminutive cooks churn out kilos of tasty pad thai every few minutes; their famous version that comes wrapped in a gossamer-thin omelette is the stuff of culinary legend.

At a restaurant called P'aor I learned how good the ubiquitous tom yum can really be. They use cow's milk and tomalley, the custardy goo that comes from inside prawn heads, to make their soup base ultra-silky: the taste of that soup is like nothing else I know. Although you have to go to Bangkok to truly understand how fantastic everything tastes, if you can't, the next best thing is to go there with me.

SERVES 4–6
AS PART OF A SHARED MEAL

60 g (2¼ oz) boiled and sliced
    pork skin
3 tablespoons crushed roasted peanuts
120 g (4½ oz) som moo fermented
    pork sausage (see glossary), sliced
3 spring onions (scallions), finely sliced
2 red Asian shallots, finely sliced
5 coriander (cilantro) sprigs,
    roughly sliced
1 handful Thai basil leaves,
    roughly sliced
1 handful mint leaves, roughly sliced
1 bunch betel leaves (see glossary),
    to serve
8 iceberg lettuce leaves, to serve

RICE BALLS

300 g (10½ oz) steamed
    jasmine rice, cooled
3 red Asian shallots, diced
4 garlic cloves, diced
1 tablespoon chilli powder
50 g (1¾ oz) desiccated
    (shredded) coconut
2 eggs, beaten
50 g (1¾ oz) potato starch
vegetable oil for deep-frying
4 red chillies
sea salt

DRESSING

3 tablespoons lime juice
2 tablespoons fish sauce
1 tablespoon sugar

CRISPY RICE BALL SALAD WITH FERMENTED PORK SAUSAGE

NAM KHAO SOM MOO

In Bangkok, if you're walking around and see carts hawking something that look like Italian arancini rice balls, drop what you're doing and order some. You'll most likely end up with this salad; it's beyond fantastic. Originating in Laos, which has much in common with the Isaan food of north-east Thailand, it's got all the bold flavours this part of the country is known for. To make the balls, cold cooked jasmine rice is mixed with dessicated coconut, shallots, chilli and garlic then bound with egg, formed into balls and fried until golden, crunchy and crispy. These get pulled apart, tossed with a pile of herbs, some pork skin and peanuts, then finished with a punchy, limey dressing. One of the best parts of this dish though is the fermented pork sausage, a speciality of Isaan. It's made by raw-curing pork with pig's skin, sticky rice, salt and chilli and the end result is deep pink and tastes deliciously sweet and porky. The idea with this dish is that, to eat it, you take a betel leaf or a lettuce leaf, put some rice ball and a bit of everything else over it along with the dressing, wrap it up then eat it with your hands.

Combine the dressing ingredients in a mixing bowl and stir until the sugar has dissolved.

To make the rice balls, put the cooled steamed rice, shallots, garlic, chilli powder, desiccated coconut and half the beaten egg in a bowl and season generously with salt. With wet hands, mix all the ingredients together well, then shape the mixture into golf ball-sized pieces. Set aside.

In a small mixing bowl, mix together the remaining beaten egg, potato starch and 2 tablespoons of water to form a light batter.

Pour enough vegetable oil for deep-frying into a wok or deep-fryer and bring to 180°C (350°F), or until a cube of bread dropped into the oil browns in 15 seconds.

Coat each rice ball with the light batter, then add to the hot oil in small batches and deep-fry for 3–4 minutes, or until golden brown and crispy. Drain on paper towels and leave to cool.

Now deep-fry the red chillies for 3 minutes or until crisp. Drain and set aside to cool.

In a large mixing bowl, break the rice balls into bite-sized pieces, then add the sliced pork skin, peanuts, fermented sausage, spring onions, shallots and herbs, and mix together well. Pour over the dressing and toss together.

Transfer the salad to a serving platter and garnish with the fried chillies. Serve with betel and iceberg lettuce leaves for wrapping and eating.

Spotting this street vendor in the Phaya Thai neighbourhood with a cart full of fried rice balls, I simply couldn't resist. I had to get behind there and make one for myself, loaded with chilli.

CRISPY FISH FLAKES & GREEN MANGO SALAD

YUM PLA DUK FOO	Soi 5, Phaya Thai	THB 50.00 AUD $2.00

A part of Bangkok I really love is the small sliver of a neighbourhood between the busy Siam and Victory Monument shopping areas in Phetchaburi called Phaya Thai. It's a small residential area, where you get a very real sense of how people in Bangkok actually live, away from all the glitzy malls and busy tourist centres. I like a street called Soi 5, where I reckon you get some of the best street food in the city. One dish I particularly like is crispy fish with green mango salad. Typically, when I arrive in town, I stumble off the MTR stop right near Soi 5 and make a beeline for it; for me, it represents everything about Thai cooking I love. There are women around here, selling this salad, with the assorted ingredients all prepared, ready to mix to order and be eaten. The crispy fish in this dish is light, textural and smoky, tossed with tart green mango, fresh herbs and lemongrass and topped with a sweet and spicy dressing. The salty/sour/spicy/sweet notes are in perfect balance. Like many Thai dishes, this one seems simple but there's actually a considerable degree of complexity behind it. The key ingredient is the crisp fried fish 'fluff'; traditionally catfish is used and it goes through a few processes. First, it's roasted before the flesh is finely flaked off the bone using a fork. Next it goes into an oven to dry out a bit, then finally it's deep-fried until it forms a fluffy, golden, crunchy mass. Even non-fish eaters will love this dish as there is nothing 'fishy' tasting about it at all – it's simply about punchy, fresh ingredients with loads of textural interest, and a particularly zingy dressing.

RED ANT & ANT EGG SALAD

KOI KHAI MOT DANG

**SERVES 4–6
AS PART OF A SHARED MEAL**

3 tablespoons red ant eggs

1 tablespoon live red ants (optional)

2 spring onions (scallions), finely sliced

1 large red onion, finely sliced

2 lemongrass stems, white part only,
   finely sliced

1 small handful coriander (cilantro)
   leaves, sliced

10 mint leaves, sliced

10 Vietnamese mint leaves, sliced

3 saw-tooth coriander (cilantro;
   see glossary) leaves, sliced

1 tablespoon fish sauce

¼ teaspoon chilli flakes

1 teaspoon Toasted Rice Powder
   (see page 292)

juice of 1 lime

10 small Chinese cabbage leaves

This is another classic Isaan dish, and also one with a heavy Laotian influence; the spicy, earthy seasonings are very northern Thai in character. Ants are actually really good to eat and if you've never been game to try them, I urge you to give them a go. As the name of this recipe suggests, you include their eggs as well as the live ants. These red ants live in trees, feed off mango leaves and as you eat them, they sort of explode in your mouth and leave a sour, fragrant, citrusy taste that's particularly unique. The eggs are soft and a little more elegant to eat, with a gorgeous, gooey texture that's hard to describe. Both ants and eggs are a great source of protein, so they're good for you as well as tasting amazing. Needless to say, there's a lot going on in this salad! You've got lemongrass, red onion and the soft pop of the eggs. Toasted rice powder, a hallmark of Isaan salads, is essential for achieving the right texture here; it's pleasantly gritty and tastes a bit biscuity.

Combine all the salad ingredients, except the cabbage leaves, in a mixing bowl. Toss together well, then transfer to a serving platter.

Serve the cabbage leaves with the salad and use them as 'spoons' to eat the salad with.

DRIED SQUID

PLA MUOK YANG	Soi 5, Phetchaburi	THB 19.00 AUD $0.75

I love eating dried squid; you see it all through South-East Asia, where it's popular as a snack at any time of the day. As I walk the streets of Bangkok in particular I often come across guys selling grilled dried squid. The stall I like most has its squid hanging so beautifully, in maybe four overlapping rows, hung up on lines with yellow, green, pink, purple and blue clothes pegs – it's so pretty. This guy uses a vintage cast-iron press to flatten his squid; it's an old hand-cranked Japanese sugar cane press and it presses squid just as effectively as it no doubt did sugar cane. Ingenious. Once the squid are totally flat, he puts each one into a wire cage, then briefly chargrills them until they're brown and wonderfully crunchy around the edges. A good time to eat these is around 6 pm, with a cold beer and sweet chilli sauce for dipping. They make the best ever drinking snack, bar none.

คลื่นความถี่
1800M

SWEET COCONUT RICE CAKES WITH TARO, CORN & SPRING ONION

KHANOM KROK

Phetchaburi Soi 5

THB 15.00 AUD $0.50

These are one of the best sweet snacks that Bangkok has to offer and, as this city is exploding with wonderful sweets, that's saying something. Part-fritter, part-pancake, part-custard, they are cooked in semi-circular depressions in a special cast-iron pan. The round indentations in the pan are said to look like a mortar, or 'krok' in Thai, hence the name khanom krok ('khanom' means 'cake' or 'dessert'). The batter is made from rice flour, glutinous rice flour and coconut cream, with a touch of sugar. When the batter is half cooked, sweet coconut milk is poured over each one, which keeps the centres soft and sweet, while the outsides cook to be crisp and brown. Then bits of taro, corn and spring onion (scallion) get sprinkled on the top; you eat them hot. Sweet, savoury, gooey, crunchy and chewy all at the same time, they're small and light and a good pick-me-up while you walk the streets of Bangkok. They're also very pretty to look at – the pans are cute and the vibrant toppings against the white cakes really make them pop.

OXTAIL SOUP

HANG WUAO	Aeesa Rot Dee, 178 Tanee Road, near Khao San Road	THB 80.00 AUD $3.00

One of my favourite hidden gems in Bangkok has to be Aeesa Rot Dee, located at 178 Tanee Road near the busy Khao San Road. It's tucked away down the darkest, narrowest laneway entrance (you could easily walk past it) but once inside, you can't help but notice the gorgeous smells and all the cooking activity. They serve the best Thai Muslim cuisine in Bangkok, I reckon, and are open from 6 am until 4 pm and then from 5 pm until 10 pm. The first aroma that hits you on arrival comes from a big pot of oxtail soup, simmering away at the front. It's a Thai dish but there are a whole pile of Indian and Middle Eastern spices like cinnamon and cardamom going on in that broth, so for an uncertain moment you're not exactly sure what country you are in. There are also a few unexpected ingredients like potatoes and tomatoes alongside the more usual Thai ones, such as saw-tooth coriander (cilantro; see glossary), fried shallots and fish sauce. I found researching Thai Muslim cuisine to be fascinating. Thailand's proximity to Indonesia and Malaysia has given rise to inevitable culinary influences from those places but, maybe not so obviously, there are also Persian links too, as Persians settled in Phuket and that community had an influence on southern Thai cuisine. Just try this soup in Bangkok and if you're not as intrigued by all of this culinary history as I am, you'll at least love the soothing, home-style flavour of it – not to mention those sticky, soft bits of oxtail.

THAI CHICKEN BIRYANI

KHAO MOK GAI	178 Tanee Road, near Khao San Road	THB 50.00 AUD $2.00

In the same laneway off Tanee Road as I find oxtail soup (see page 233), I also eat some of the best Thai-style chicken biryani in Bangkok. Past the damp, dark entrance, a vast interior opens up that's filled with shafts of sunlight. It's spartan and looks a bit like a gym but it's actually really peaceful and calm in here. Down the left side is a whole lot of ready-prepared food and you just point to what you fancy, take it to one of the 10 or so tables, pull up a plastic chair and eat. It's busy in here, with endless streams of Bangkok's Muslims coming in for a halal meal. Khao mok gai is arguably the most famous Thai Muslim dish of all. It's full of flavours from neighbouring Malaysia and Indonesia but with Indian influences as well – essentially, this is a type of biryani, a very subcontinental dish. People argue endlessly about where it came from – northern India or even Persia. Traditionally in Thailand it was cooked for large functions such as weddings but today you can find it easily at Muslim street food stalls across Bangkok. It's got a really complex set of exotic flavours – when you eat this, you almost feel like you are no longer in Bangkok, that's for sure. You could be in the Middle East. I love how food has that power to transport you somewhere else.

MAKES 50

25 x 22 cm (8½ in) spring roll papers
    (about 1 packet)
1 teaspoon plain (all-purpose) flour
    mixed with 1 tablespoon water
vegetable oil for deep-frying

FILLING

80 g (3 oz) glass noodles
50 g (1¾ oz) dried black fungus strips
    (wood ears; see glossary)
400 g (14 oz) minced (ground) chicken
100 g (3½ oz) carrots, grated
150 g (5½ oz) taro, peeled and grated
½ onion, finely diced
1 tablespoon sugar
3 teaspoons salt
2 teaspoons fine white pepper
1 tablespoon fish sauce

TO SERVE

25 mustard green leaves (see glossary)
    or butter lettuce leaves
1 bunch mint leaves
1 bunch Thai basil leaves
250 ml (9 fl oz/1 cup) Nuoc Cham,
    to serve (see page 90)

CHICKEN, TARO &
GLASS NOODLE SPRING ROLLS

POR PIA TOD

I'm still in the Muslim eatery off Tanee Road and at every turn I feel like this food is taking me to a different part of the world. In a lovely sunlit spot I see a man making spring rolls, which he stacks so beautifully, forming a perfect pyramid of them on a big tray. I'm reminded that this might 'just' be street food, but people take such great care with it, and have incredible pride in everything they produce. These spring rolls make me feel like I could be in Saigon – they're very similar to what I eat there. They're halal though, so chicken is used for the filling, amped up with some glass noodles, carrot and taro, and seasoned with sugar, white pepper and fish sauce.

Just like in Vietnam, you eat these deep-fried morsels wrapped, with herbs, in a mustard green leaf and dunked into nuoc cham. Mustard green leaves have a great peppery flavour but at home you can just use butter lettuce leaves if you prefer. Once prepared, the spring rolls can be stored in the freezer and cooked when required; from frozen, they will take 7–8 minutes to cook.

For the filling, soak the noodles and mushroom strips separately in cold water for 20 minutes, then drain and dry. Cut the noodles into 4 cm (1½ in) lengths, then combine with the remaining filling ingredients in a large bowl and mix well.

Arrange the spring roll papers in a stack and cut diagonally to form two triangles, then separate the papers into single sheets.

Place one spring roll paper on a plate with the base of the triangle facing you. Spoon a tablespoon of the mixture onto the centre of the base edge, then fold the two adjacent sides, one on top of the other into the centre to cover. Now roll up the sheet away from you towards the tip of the triangle to form a nice firm roll and secure with a dab of flour mixed with some water. Repeat until you have filled all of the papers.

Pour enough vegetable oil for deep-frying into a wok or deep-fryer and bring to 180°C (350°F), or until a cube of bread dropped into the oil browns in 15 seconds. Add the spring rolls to the hot oil in small batches and deep-fry for 4–5 minutes, or until golden brown and crisp. Drain on paper towels.

Serve hot, wrapped in the lettuce and herb leaves, with a bowl of nuoc cham for dipping.

STEAMED RICE NOODLES WITH DRIED SHRIMP, MUSHROOM & TOFU

KUAI TEAW LORD	Yaowarat Road, Chinatown	THB 25.00 AUD $1.00

Walking through the old streets of Bangkok, I come across a woman with a large steamer tray. Curious to see what is under the lid, I open it and find a selection of cute little bamboo baskets filled with thick, pinkish rice noodles, flecked with speckles of dried shrimp (see glossary). Of course, I have to order one to see what she creates. On doing so, the vendor empties the hot noodles onto a bed of crunchy bean sprouts, then tops them with sliced fresh mint and coriander (cilantro). She then ladles over a combination of Asian mushrooms, Chinese sausage and firm tofu that has been simmering away in a dark soy sauce. Fried garlic and dried chilli flakes are sprinkled on top for garnish, with the lot finished off with a drizzle of sweet soy sauce. Delicious. Eating this incredibly tasty and well-executed dish, I can hardly believe that I have just discovered it on a roadside, instead of a great restaurant.

DRY RICE NOODLES WITH ROASTED PORK & CRACKLING

KUAI TEAW SUKOTHAI	Soi Wat Sangwech, Phra Athit Road, Banglamphu	THB 40.00 AUD $1.50

On Phra Athit Road in Bangkok's old town, Banglamphu, I come across another very local haunt. It's a little shop-house that cooks traditional, old-school Thai dishes that are hard to find elsewhere; many are from the Chinese Thai repertoire. Only locals seem to know about it and when you come here in the morning, the owners address everyone in the queue by their first name. This neighbourhood is quiet, everyone is super friendly and they make you feel like you are inside someone's home, not in a restaurant. The people here are so welcoming and their dishes, so everyone tells me, are ones I'll struggle to find elsewhere in Bangkok. They urge me to try this, which they are actually quite famous for – the Sukothai in the name points to the ancient Thai capital of Sukothai, nearly 400 kilometres to the north of Bangkok, where this dish originated. It's a rice noodle dish which you order with your preference of noodles; either 'sen lek' (medium-sized noodles like the ones that go into pad thai) or 'sen lee' (thin noodles like angel hair). Both types are springy and nicely al dente and come with roasted pork and crisp pork crackling on top. The noodles can be served either dry, as I have them, or in clear stock. When soupy, the dish is basically a Chinese-style noodle soup with distinctively Thai seasonings. Either dry or soupy, you get loads of bean sprouts, roast pork, peanuts and lovely, crisp, deep-fried pieces of pork crackling. The cooks here season the noodles with chilli flakes, vinegar and sugar and throw some coriander (cilantro) in too. A squeeze of lime, and that's it.

THAI RICE NOODLES WITH PINEAPPLE & COCONUT MILK

KHANOM JEEN SAO NAM	Somsong Pochana, Phra Athit Road, Banglamphu	THB 50.00 AUD $2.00

A discovery I make at the fabulous Somsong Pochana is khanom jeen sao nam, or fine, fermented rice noodles with pineapple and coconut milk. Khanom jeen are the only noodles the Thai eat with curries and you can find them served in various ways all over Bangkok. But this dish is not so common. The thin noodles, which have to be eaten the day they are made, go on a plate together with bits of young ginger, fine julienned pineapple and a sprinkling of salty dried prawn chopped so fine it's almost like floss. Next, on goes a whole spoonful of sugar, plenty of rich, creamy coconut milk, a few squirts of fresh lime juice and some chopped green and red chillies, too. The noodles soak in all the sharp, sweet, creamy, fresh flavours; this dish looks rich but it's actually light and cooling. The star of the dish is the beautifully buttery and thick coconut milk that contrasts with all the other flavours. Go to this place and order a plateful – they sell it all year round.

CRISPY VERMICELLI NOODLES

MEE KROB	Mit Ko Yuan, Dinso Road, Sao Chingcha	THB 50.00 AUD $2.00

If you're up near the Giant Swing or the Democracy Monument, you must dine at Mit Ko Yuan on Dinso Road in Sao Chingcha. I'm telling you, this place has not changed a bit since it opened over 60 years ago. They've still got the original decor so it's truly olde-worlde, with tiled walls, blue shelves and gorgeous old wooden tables and stools down each side. It oozes character. Despite being wildly popular they've never expanded and they even run the same menu they had when they opened – there's a copy of it on the wall complete with the original prices. I love their mee krob, which is basically a plate of deep-fried vermicelli noodles coated in an unbelievably delicious sauce. You'll see mee krob cooked on the street too, a process which normally involves two cooks. One deep-fries the noodles in a massive wok, the other looks after the lovely thick, sweet, sour and spicy sauce – usually made from tamarind, tomato, fish sauce, onion and palm sugar – in another big wok. The noodles are deep-fried for a split second only and it's an incredible process to watch as they puff up straight away, like prawn crackers. Next, they're drained then added immediately to the second wok where they're cooked until they 'wilt' a bit and absorb plenty of that delicious sweet-and-sour sauce. The dish is then garnished with chillies, bean sprouts, herbs, fresh shaved coconut and lime juice.

CHARGRILLED SPICY PRAWN SALAD

GOONG PLA

SERVES 4–6
AS PART OF A SHARED MEAL

500 g (1 lb 2 oz) raw king prawns
     (shrimp), peeled and deveined,
     heads and tails intact
1 tablespoon Thai roasted red chilli
     paste (see glossary)
1 handful coriander (cilantro)
     sprigs, torn
1 handful mint leaves
1 handful Thai basil leaves
4 makrut (kaffir lime) leaves,
     finely sliced
4 cm (1½ in) lemongrass stalk,
     white part only, very finely sliced
4 red Asian shallots, finely sliced

DRESSING
1 tablespoon sugar
2 tablespoons fish sauce
3 tablespoons lime juice
2 tablespoons Thai roasted red chilli
     paste (see glossary)
3–5 bird's eye chillies, sliced

Here's another dish which is really very simple and one I particularly like to order at Mit Ko Yuan. Hot-and-sour salads like this are at the heart of Thai cuisine and you can balance the chilli and lime juice to suit your own taste. Here, the prawns are the star. They use gorgeously fresh chargrilled king prawns for this salad, serving them in their charred shells. I notice they deliberately undercook them; they're what I'd call 'rare'. I love them this way; the flesh is butter-soft and ridiculously sweet but this approach only works with super-fresh prawns. If you like your prawns like this too, then cook them for about a minute on each side, making sure you've got your grill very, very hot so you still get that charred, smoky flavour. If you're dubious about underdone prawns, remember that they go into a lime-heavy dressing and the acid keeps cooking them, even once they're off the heat.

Put the prawns in a mixing bowl, add the chilli paste and stir to coat them well. Leave to marinate for 15 minutes.

Meanwhile, combine the dressing ingredients in a bowl and stir until the sugar is dissolved.

Heat a chargrill pan or barbecue chargrill to medium–high. Cook the prawns for 2–3 minutes on each side until golden and cooked through.

Add the chargrilled prawns to a mixing bowl with the coriander, mint, Thai basil, makrut leaves, lemongrass, shallots and dressing. Toss together well, transfer to a plate and serve.

**SERVES 4-6
AS PART OF A SHARED MEAL**

1 x 400 g (14 oz) small
    whole raw lobster, cleaned
1 tablespoon salt
1 litre (35 fl oz/4 cups) Prawn Head
    Stock (see page 293)
2 lemongrass stems,
    white part only, bruised
3 cm (1¼ in) piece of fresh galangal,
    finely sliced
4 bird's eye chillies, bruised
3 red Asian shallots,
    peeled and bruised
4 makrut (kaffir lime) leaves, torn
4 tablespoons fish sauce
3 tablespoons Thai roasted
    red chilli paste (see glossary)
150 ml (5 fl oz) evaporated milk
5 cherry tomatoes, quartered
2 spring onions (scallions),
    cut into 4 cm (1½ in) lengths
3 saw-tooth coriander (cilantro;
    see glossary) leaves, sliced
juice of 2 limes
1 hard-boiled egg, halved
100 g (3½ oz) rice vermicelli noodles,
    cooked according to packet
    instructions
1 handful coriander (cilantro),
    to garnish

LOBSTER TOM YUM

TOM YUM GOONG MUNG KOR

Phetchaburi Soi 5... Remember this address, because you seriously want to come here when you travel to Bangkok – it's got one of the best concentrations of street food in the entire city. Plus, the residential neighbourhood around here has a particularly nice, authentic vibe. There's a great (and wildly popular) restaurant called P'aor, in an old shop-house. As you walk in, you notice hefty pots simmering away, filled with a deep orange-red broth that looks for all the world like a French seafood bisque. Except you know it's not when the whiffs of lemongrass, galangal, chillies and makrut leaves start to take hold. It's actually tom yum and while I've had a lot of tom yum in my time, it's never been anything like this. It's not clear, as tom yum usually is, but rather rich and creamy and I find out their secret is in stirring tomalley – which is essentially the custard-like goo found in prawn and lobster heads – and tinned evaporated milk into the soup. Lobster makes the dish even more lavish and special. By the way, P'aor cook plenty of other amazing things but their tom yum, unique in Bangkok, is definitely their signature. The serve is so enormous (you get an entire lobster, plus stuffed squid, stuffed crab, mussels, salmon and boiled egg) that you can easily share it among two or even three people – it's a dish and a half. This version has been pared back a bit, but is no less delicious.

Place the lobster on a chopping board. Using a pair of sharp kitchen scissors and starting at the tail end, cut the lobster in half lengthways through the tough outer shell.

Cover the base of a stockpot, saucepan or steamer with 4 cm (1½ in) of water and stir in 1 tablespoon of salt to dissolve, then add a steamer basket to the pan and bring the water to the boil over a high heat. Add the lobster halves to the pan head first, cover with a lid, and steam for 8 minutes (the lobster will only be partially cooked at this point and will finish cooking in the stock later). Remove from the pan and set aside.

Add the stock, lemongrass, galangal, chillies, shallots and makrut leaves to a stockpot or large saucepan. Bring to the boil, then reduce the heat and simmer for 5 minutes. Stir in the fish sauce, Thai roasted red chilli paste, evaporated milk and simmer for another 2–3 minutes, then add the lobster and cherry tomatoes and return to the boil.

Skim off any impurities from the surface of the broth, then reduce the heat to low and simmer for 6 minutes, or until the lobster is just cooked. Stir in the spring onion, saw-tooth coriander, lime juice and hard-boiled egg halves.

To serve, place the vermicelli noodles in a large serving bowl. Remove the lobster halves from the broth and place on top of the noodles, then ladle over the broth until the noodles are fully submerged. Garnish with coriander and serve.

**SERVES 4-6
AS PART OF A SHARED MEAL**

2 potatoes, peeled and cut into
    3 cm (1¼ inch) chunks
1 tablespoon vegetable oil
2 garlic cloves, diced
2 cm (¾ in) piece of fresh ginger,
    finely sliced
4 red Asian shallots, diced
1 teaspoon red curry powder
450 g (1 lb) boneless, skinless
    chicken thighs, cut into 3 cm
    (1¼ inch) chunks
125 ml (4 fl oz/½ cup) Chicken Stock
    (see page 214)
1 tablespoon liquid palm sugar
    (see glossary) or shaved
    palm sugar (jaggery)
3 tablespoons light soy sauce
1 tablespoon fish sauce
165 ml (5½ fl oz) coconut milk
1 tablespoon kecap manis
    (see glossary)
2 red chillies, sliced
2 green chillies, sliced

CURRY PASTE

4 dried red chillies, soaked in hot
    water for 10 minutes, then drained
    and chopped
4 red Asian shallots, chopped
4 garlic cloves, chopped
2 lemongrass stalks,
    white part only, sliced
4 cm (1½ in) piece of fresh ginger,
    peeled and sliced
4 coriander (cilantro) stalks,
    scraped clean and chopped
1 teaspoon shrimp paste
½ teaspoon ground cumin
½ teaspoon ground coriander
½ teaspoon ground white pepper
½ teaspoon paprika
pinch of sea salt

CHINATOWN RED CHICKEN & POTATO CURRY

KAREE GAI

Close to the famous Dragon Flower Temple on Mangkorn Road in Bangkok's Chinatown you'll find one of the city's best street food stalls, Jek Pui. The current owner was set up by his father, who started the stall, and all the cooking is done in a small house just around the corner, about 15 metres away. Two workers transfer massive pots full of cooked food down the street, from the kitchen to the stall, using a sturdy bamboo pole. They specialise in curry and have every type you could imagine; green, yellow, red, pork, chicken and beef. Oh, and they also serve a braised spicy pork rib dish too. Before lining up to order, you must know what you want – if you are indecisive and stall even for a nanosecond, they will kick you out of the line. When you get your curry you sit on a stool, sandwiched between that fantastic old wall and the street, with all the locals, curry balanced on your knee. No tables. There are accompaniments like kecap manis, chilli sauce, chillies and vinegar to add; you find these on plastic stools and if you're not sure what, when or how to add, just follow the locals' lead. Coming here is a spectacular experience, I promise you. Oh and I should mention the actual curry! Jek Pui's curries are a lot lighter than what you might be familiar with or may be expecting from a Thai curry. The flavours are subtle, and won't blow your head off with chilli heat. The karee gai is a favourite of mine; it's red, instead of the more common green, and is southern Thai in style, with aromatic dried spices like coriander and cumin seeds used in the paste. As well as curry paste they use curry powder, which somehow lightens the whole thing. When you dine here you can easily fit in two serves; they are also famous for their kaeng karee, which involves either pork or beef, is creamy, made with curry powder and is probably Chinese Thai in origin. Whatever you order, be sure to get an iced tea to go with it; there's nowhere to put it, so it just goes on the ground.

For the curry paste, pound all the ingredients together in a mortar and pestle to a smooth paste. Set aside.

Bring a saucepan of water to the boil over a high heat. Add the potatoes and boil for 5 minutes. Drain and set aside.

Heat a saucepan over a medium–high heat. Add the vegetable oil and sauté the garlic, ginger and shallots for 2 minutes until fragrant. Stir in the red curry paste and curry powder and cook for 1 minute, then add the chicken thigh pieces and stir-fry for 2–3 minutes, or until slightly browned.

Stir in the chicken stock, palm sugar, light soy sauce, fish sauce, coconut milk and potatoes. Bring to the boil, then reduce the heat and simmer for 8–10 minutes, until the liquid has reduced slightly and the flavours have melded together.

Transfer to a serving bowl and drizzle with the kecap manis. Garnish with the sliced red and green chillies and serve.

RICE PASTA WITH ROAST PORK, OFFAL & WHITE PEPPER BROTH

KUAI JAP NAM SAI	Nai Lek, Yaowarat Road, Soi 11	THB 50.00 AUD $2.00

Right on an intersection on Yaowarat Road, at the entrance to the old market on Soi 11, you'll find what has to be one of the busiest street food stalls in the whole of Chinatown. People are known to cross town to come here. Called Nai Lek, it's open Tuesday to Sunday from about 6.30 pm; it doesn't close until midnight and there are constant, and long, queues of punters waiting for a serve of the famous kuai jap. It's a rice noodle dish but I think of the noodles more as a kind of 'pasta' as, before they're cooked, they look like bits of unstuffed ravioli. The minute they hit boiling water, the noodles curl; they're retrieved while still al dente. They get served in a broth loaded with offal (pork heart, liver, stomach and tongue), roast pork and pork crackling. The textures are something special, a mix of toothsome, slippery and soft; but it's the clear broth that's the real hero for me. The strong flavour comes from plenty of white pepper and it lends a taste that really lingers, long after you've eaten a bowl. The family that run this stall have been making kuai jap for years and it is the only thing they serve. So it's fair to say they've perfected everything about this dish, right down to the subtlest nuances of flavour.

There was so much talent and passion on display at this restaurant. I just stood back on the road side, admiring the skills of all the chefs, tossing, firing, flipping and serving hundreds of dishes of their famous pad thai.

PAD THAI WITH EGG WRAP

PHAD THAI HOR KAI

Pad thai is so famous – maybe the most famous of all Thai dishes – that initially I was hesitant to discuss it. Then I discovered Thip Samai. I am blown away by this place, where pad thai is the speciality and they make a few different variants. By far the most interesting is the one that comes wrapped in fine egg omelette. You find the restaurant at 511 Mahachai Road, in a slightly quieter part of the city and you can't miss it. Just look for the bonfires of wok flames out the front of the restaurant, where the cooking stations are. The first thing to know is that Thip Samai is always super busy. The cooks move at warp speed in a blur of flames and smoke, sending noodles literally flying, to keep up with the constant demand from in-house diners and customers swooping by for takeaway. I love watching the cooks at work. They cook maybe ten serves at a time and I reckon a fully loaded wok must weigh around 20 kilos. Once a batch of pad thai is cooked, on goes another; it's an endless process, involving awe-inspiring speed and skill, that continues without break until they close at 2 am. To make the pad thai sauce they crush prawn heads to extract the tomalley, or juices, within. This gives wonderful flavour to the noodles; as a chef I respect little refinements like this. What's really amazing to watch is how they make the omelette wrapping for the phad thai hor kai. Dozens of portions of cooked noodles are transported to chefs using smaller woks, who make one thin omelette after another. As each omelette cooks, they throw in a portion of the cooked noodles, deftly flipping the whole thing so the noodles are enclosed in omelette. Thip Samai is an essential food destination in Bangkok, but you can make the omelette pad thai at home – it's not complicated. Be sure to use the right, thin flat rice noodles – definitely not vermicelli noodles!

2 eggs, at room temperature
4 tablespoons vegetable oil
3 garlic cloves, diced
3 red Asian shallots, diced
10 raw medium-sized tiger prawns
    (shrimp), peeled and deveined
    with tails intact
1 tablespoon dried shrimp
    (see glossary), soaked in warm
    water for 15 minutes, then drained
100 g (3½ oz) very firm tofu, drained
    and cut into 2 cm (¾ in) cubes
200 g (7 oz) flat rice noodles,
    soaked in water for 20 minutes,
    then drained
6 garlic chives, sliced into 4 cm
    (1½ in) lengths
90 g (3¼ oz/1 cup) bean sprouts
2 tablespoons crushed roasted peanuts
¼ teaspoon dried chilli flakes,
    for sprinkling
2 coriander (cilantro) sprigs, to garnish
sea salt

SAUCE
125 ml (4 fl oz/½ cup) Tamarind Water
    (see page 152)
4 tablespoons fish sauce
2½ tablespoons liquid palm sugar
    (see glossary) or shaved
    palm sugar (jaggery)

TO SERVE
1 lime, cut into wedges
90 g (3¼ oz/1 cup) bean sprouts
4 garlic chives, cut in half
4 red chillies, sliced and mixed with
    2 tablespoons fish sauce (optional)

Combine the sauce ingredients together with 80 ml (3 fl oz/⅓ cup) water in a small saucepan over a medium heat. Stir until the palm sugar dissolves, then transfer to a small bowl and set aside.

Beat the eggs together in a bowl and season with a pinch of salt. Set aside.

Add 2 tablespoons of the vegetable oil to a hot wok and heat until smoking. Add the garlic and shallots and stir-fry for 30 seconds until fragrant. Add the prawns and stir-fry for 1 minute, then add the dried shrimp, tofu, noodles and sauce. Toss for 2 minutes, then add the garlic chives and bean sprouts and toss for another minute. Transfer to a mixing bowl and cover to keep warm. Set aside.

Wipe the wok clean and place back over a medium–high heat. Add the remaining vegetable oil, ensuring it coats the surface of the wok evenly. Taking hold of the handle with one hand, pour in the beaten egg, then quickly swirl the wok in a wide circular motion, coating the sides of the wok and creating a very thin crêpe-like layer of egg. Cook for 1 minute, or until the egg 'crêpe' is set.

Spoon the cooked noodle mixture into the centre of the wok and scatter over the peanuts, then fold over the sides of egg 'crêpe' into the centre to cover the noodles and form a parcel. Flip the egg-wrapped pad thai over in the wok to briefly seal the folded ends, then slide it onto a serving plate.

Garnish with the chilli flakes and coriander sprigs and serve with lime wedges, bean sprouts, garlic chives, and a mixture of chilli slices and fish sauce.

**Drunken
Noodles
with Prawns**
*Phad Kee
Mao Goong*

258 >

SERVES 2

2 tablespoons vegetable oil

3 garlic cloves, diced

2 long red chillies, finely sliced

8 large raw prawns (shrimp), peeled
and deveined with tails intact

200 g (7 oz) flat rice noodles,
soaked in water for 20 minutes,
then drained

6 baby corn, halved lengthways

6 button mushrooms, halved

2 spring onions (scallions),
sliced into 3 cm (1¼ in) lengths

1 handful Thai basil leaves

SAUCE

3 tablespoons oyster sauce

1 tablespoon light soy sauce

2 teaspoons dark soy sauce

2 teaspoons liquid palm sugar
(see glossary) or shaved
palm sugar (jaggery)

2 tablespoons hot water

DRUNKEN NOODLES
WITH PRAWNS

PHAD KEE MAO GOONG

Jay Fai is a no-frills eatery in a shop-house that's very close to Thip Samai at 327 Mahachai Road. It's hardly a new find; every Asian food expert and writer there knows this place. My favourite dish here is drunken noodles but I love the chef-owner even more. Her name is also Jay Fai (although she's variously called 'old auntie' or 'grandmother') and she tells me she's been cooking for 60 years and has never taken a sick day in her life. It's amazing to watch her in the kitchen; she wears a brown beanie and covers her eyes with what look like 1950s flying goggles to protect them from all the smoke and flying sparks. At any one time she has three woks on the go and, as she cooks over charcoal, there are plenty of dramatic flames. Hers is said to be the most expensive street food in all of Bangkok and this comes down to the quality of her ingredients – she doesn't compromise or cut corners. Her seafood, for example, is top notch and her famous drunken noodles feature the freshest, fattest, sweetest prawns imaginable. She cranks the heat up to the absolute maximum so the noodles get that lovely scorched flavour. Incidentally, there are various stories told about why this dish is called 'drunken', even though it contains no alcohol. I'm told it's because the dish has so much intense flavour that you feel a bit buzzed-up and drunk after eating it. Who knows? It's delicious, whatever the theory.

Combine the sauce ingredients in a small mixing bowl with 2 tablespoons of hot water and stir until the palm sugar has dissolved. Set aside.

Heat a wok until smoking hot. Add the vegetable oil and heat until smoking, then add the garlic and red chilli and stir-fry for 30 seconds until fragrant.

Add the prawns and stir-fry for another minute, then add the noodles, baby corn, mushrooms, spring onions and sauce and toss for 2 minutes, or until the vegetables are cooked and all the sauce has been absorbed by the noodles.

Remove the wok from the heat, add the Thai basil and toss together, then transfer to individual plates and serve.

THREE-COLOURED STICKY RICE WITH SWEET MANGO

KHAO NIEW MAMUANG

SERVES 4–6

1 bunch (50 g/1¾ oz) magenta leaves,
  coarsely chopped
1 bunch (50 g/1¾ oz) pandan leaves
  (see glossary), roughly chopped
500 g (1 lb 2 oz/3 cups) sticky
  (glutinous) rice
115 g (4 oz/½ cup) sugar
1 tablespoon salt
1 tablespoon vegetable oil
4 ripe sweet mangoes, peeled and
  sliced into 3 cm (1¼ in) widths

SWEET COCONUT MILK DRESSING
500 ml (18 fl oz/2 cups) coconut milk
125 ml (4 fl oz/½ cup) liquid
  palm sugar (see glossary) or
  shaved palm sugar (jaggery)
½ teaspoon sea salt

CRISPY MUNG BEANS
4 tablespoons vegetable oil
90 g (3¼ oz/1 cup) dried mung beans,
  soaked in water for 15 minutes,
  then drained and patted dry

On the bucket list of just about every tourist to Thailand is a visit to a floating market. If you don't want to get up too early, there's Talin Chan, just 12 kilometres out of town – it's a bit lacking in authentic charm but there's some great food here, such as this dish, which I really hope you try. Now, I know mango with sticky rice is a well-known Thai snack but at Talin Chan there's a lady who makes it with coloured rice. So when you order hers, you get a pile each of green sticky rice (tinted with pandan leaf), purple sticky rice (coloured using magenta leaves, which can be found at good Asian grocers) and plain rice, garnished with fried mung beans. The mangoes are fat and juicy and the way she prepares them, to order, is pretty impressive. She passes you the dish in a basket on a long bamboo stick from her boat. You take your dish then put money in the basket to pay her. It's really great fun.

In a small saucepan, combine 500 ml (18 fl oz/2 cups) water with the magenta leaves. Bring to a boil, reduce the heat to medium–low, cover and simmer for 10 minutes. Turn off the heat and let it steep for 30 minutes. Drain the purple water into a bowl and discard the leaves.

Meanwhile, place the pandan leaves in a blender with 375 ml (13 fl oz/1½ cups) water and blend for 2 minutes until a green liquid forms. Transfer to a mixing bowl then, with your hands, squeeze the pandan pulp extracting all the green liquid. Discard the pulp. Rinse the sticky rice with cold water and drain.

Divide the rice into thirds and add to separate deep mixing bowls. Submerge one third of the rice with the extracted purple water, another third with the extracted green water and the final third with regular water. Add a pinch of salt to each bowl and soak the rice at room temperature for at least 6 hours, or overnight. The sticky rice will expand slightly, so check it after 2 hours to make sure it is still fully submerged, topping up the waters as needed.

Separately drain the three bowls of sticky rice well, but DO NOT rinse.

Add the purple rice to a Thai rice bamboo steamer basket with 2 tablespoons sugar, 1 teaspoon salt and 1 teaspoon vegetable oil. Mix, then make a small well in the middle to help the hot steam circulate. Bring a pot of water to a boil, place the steamer basket on top, cover and steam for 18–20 minutes, or until soft. Once cooked, remove from the heat, fluff up the rice, then transfer to a bowl. Cover and set aside. Repeat with first the green and then the plain white rice.

To make the dressing, add the coconut milk to a heavy-based saucepan over a medium heat and warm until hot but not boiling. Add the palm sugar and salt and stir to dissolve completely. Set aside.

For the crispy mung beans, heat the oil in a wok to a medium heat. Carefully add the mung beans and fry for 5 minutes, or until crisp. Remove from the oil, drain and leave to cool, then transfer to a bowl and season with salt. Set aside.

To serve, divide the sticky rices in scoopfuls between four serving plates. Arrange the sliced mangoes alongside the rice then pour 2 tablespoons of the sweet coconut milk dressing over each serving. Garnish with the crispy mung beans.

Three-
coloured
Sticky
Rice with
Sweet Mango
*Khao Niew
Mamuang*

< 259

BOAT NOODLES

KUAI TEAW MOO NAM TOK	Amphawa Floating Market	THB 25.00 AUD $1.00

If you want a really authentic floating market experience, be prepared to get up at 5 am for a long drive; I'd suggest hiring a car and a driver for the day. It's actually not too expensive at around AUD$80. You have to go to Amphawa Floating Market, about 90 kilometres southwest of Bangkok, where the city's natives flock during the weekend. It's vibrant, busy and the food is spectacular, especially the seafood. But I also like eating boat noodles; they're such an iconic dish. They're so-called as they originated in the floating markets and canal ways of Bangkok during the 1940s as part of a government initiative to increase noodle consumption – there was a severe rice shortage at the time and it's believed that many of Thailand's now-famous noodle dishes sprang up during this era. Traditionally, they feature a distinctive brown stock that's coloured using pig's or cow's blood, which also gives the broth its particular texture. You can still find the dish made this way but not all cooks use blood. Other ingredients and flavours, which tend to be strong, include cinnamon, dark soy, fermented tofu, pork or beef, bean sprouts, water spinach (morning glory), fried garlic, soft-boiled eggs and crisp pork rinds. It's a powerful tasting dish and one that always comes in a rather dainty portion; it's more than possible to eat two or even three bowls. The reason the bowl is so small is because decades ago, boat noodle vendors were one-man bands who had to blanch noodles, chop ingredients, assemble and serve soup, take money, give change *and* wash bowls, practically at the same time. For ease, they kept the bowls small.

CHILLI & BASIL CHICKEN WITH STEAMED RICE

PAD KRAPAO GAI

**SERVES 4–6
AS PART OF A SHARED MEAL**

6 garlic cloves
4 red Asian shallots
4 Thai red chillies
1 tablespoon vegetable oil
400 g (14 oz) boneless, skinless
   chicken breast, cut into 3 cm
   (1¼ inch) chunks
2 makrut (kaffir lime) leaves,
   finely sliced
1 large handful holy basil or
   Thai basil leaves
¼ teaspoon white pepper
steamed jasmine rice, to serve

SAUCE
1 tablespoon oyster sauce
1 tablespoon fish sauce
1 teaspoon light soy sauce
1 teaspoon sugar
1 teaspoon sweet dark soy sauce

This is another dish that grabs my attention at Amphawa Floating Market, where I smell the wonderful aroma long before I see it being cooked. I always try to eat this when I'm in Thailand – it's a classic stir-fry that's also made using pork and is generally not hard to find. The star ingredient is holy basil which is very different in character to sweeter Thai basil; spicy, a little sharp, peppery and zesty, it has distinctive anise-like overtones. It's always used in cooked dishes, unlike Thai basil which can be used raw in salads. Holy basil is just too strong. The leaf has little jagged edges and the stems are a bit purplish and you'll find it in Thai or other general Asian food stores in the fresh produce section. Using a mortar and pestle to grind up the ingredients, rather than a food processor, is important as this properly releases all the oils and juices from the chillies, garlic and shallots, and gives the finished dish a real depth of flavour.

Using a mortar and pestle, pound the garlic, shallots and chillies to a rough paste. Set aside.

Combine the sauce ingredients in a small bowl and mix until the sugar has dissolved.

Heat a wok until smoking hot. Add the vegetable oil and sauté the garlic, shallot and chilli paste for 1 minute, then add the chicken pieces and stir-fry for 2 minutes or until lightly browned. Pour over the sauce and stir-fry for a further minute.

Stir in the sliced makrut leaves, basil and white pepper, transfer to a serving platter and serve with steamed jasmine rice.

**SERVES 4–6
AS PART OF A SHARED MEAL**

12 scallops on the half-shell,
   roes removed
2 tablespoons quality unsalted butter
3 tablespoons Spring Onion Oil
   (see page 91)
3 tablespoons crushed roasted peanuts
sea salt
freshly ground black pepper

CHARGRILLED SCALLOPS WITH BUTTER & SPRING ONION OIL

HOY SHALL YANG

I can't tell you how much I enjoy Amphawa Floating Market – it's so entertaining. There's plenty of cooking action and watching the (mostly) women cook fresh seafood, with their pots, steamers, portable barbecues and other gear balanced so precariously inside tiny boats, is magical. Set along a canal lined with charming old wooden shops, it's a hot weekend destination for Bangkok-ites so you need to be prepared for major crowds. Everyone sits on the steps that lead down to the canal to watch the action and eat and what I love about this is, not only do you get to feel like a local, but you've got a ringside seat to all the cooking activity too. These scallops are a favourite of mine, especially with a cold beer. They're grilled in the half-shell, with just a little bit of butter, some peanuts and spring onion oil. They're so simple to make but, like all simple things, they rely on the freshest produce you can get your hands on in order to really shine.

Heat a barbecue chargrill or chargrill pan to a medium heat.

Season the scallops with salt and pepper, then top each piece with ½ teaspoon of the butter.

Sit the scallops in their shells on top of the hot grill and drizzle over the spring onion oil. Leave to cook for 1 minute, then sprinkle over the crushed peanuts and chargrill for a further 2 minutes, or until the scallops are just cooked through.

Transfer the scallops to a platter and serve immediately.

WAFER-THIN SWEETS WITH EGG FLOSS & DRIED SHRIMP

KHANOM BUEANG	Golden Buddha Temple, Soi Sukon 1	THB 40.00 AUD $1.50 (for 10)

I love these things! I don't just love eating them (although they are a favourite Thai sweet snack of mine), I also love watching them being made. This requires real skill plus perfect timing and to me, they're the kind of thing I'd pay serious money for in a fine-dining restaurant, rather than a few baht on the hot streets of Bangkok. This dish dates back 600 years so it's fair to say the Thais have perfected it over a long time. The batter is made using rice flour, pea flour, some palm sugar, eggs, water and a pinch of salt. It's spread to form small, super-thin discs on a hot plate; they look like tiny tacos. Once the rounds are brown and super-crisp, they're topped with an egg white and coconut sugar mixture that's been whipped until it's stiff and resembles meringue, or a mixture of dried shrimp (see glossary), grated coconut and fine threads of egg yolk called 'foi thong', or 'golden strands', with chopped coriander (cilantro) finishing the whole thing off. Buying a combo of the two, as is normal, delivers a mix of sweet and savoury flavours that may sound weird but I promise you khanom bueang taste amazing. They're not something you could easily make at home; best you get yourself to Bangkok and eat them there. My recommended place for these is near the famous Golden Buddha Temple, on Soi Sukon 1. This little street is a great daytime street food destination, kicking off with all sorts of goodies at around 11 am, just in time for lunch.

**Oyster
Omelette**
Hoy Tod

OYSTER OMELETTE

HOY TOD

35 g (1¼ oz/¼ cup) plain
    (all-purpose) flour
75 g (2¾ oz/½ cup) tapioca flour
1 teaspoon baking powder
pinch of salt
4 tablespoons vegetable oil
250 g (9 oz) raw oyster meat
2 eggs
1 tablespoon sriracha chilli sauce
4 coriander (cilantro) sprigs, to garnish

TOPPING
1 tablespoon vegetable oil
2 garlic cloves, diced
200 g (7 oz) bean sprouts
2 spring onions (scallions), sliced
1 tablespoon fish sauce
pinch of white pepper

Also near the Golden Buddha Temple is a famous little restaurant called Nai Mong Hoy Tod that specialises in oyster omelette. Now, if you've been to Bangkok but haven't had this dish, you haven't really been to Bangkok. Actually more like an eggy pancake, this omelette needs serious heat and oil to cook perfectly, although nothing about this is hard. You can definitely make it at home. On the street they use a big, heavy flat-iron plate; onto this goes plenty of oil then the batter, raw oysters, fish sauce and some bean sprouts. The whole thing cooks until it's super crisp and deep golden on the base, but still soft and gooey in the middle. As it cooks it gets broken up into rough pieces with a spatula and constantly turned – this is to render as much of the exterior as possible crispy. It's served with chilli sauce and is so addictive, it's unbelievable.

In a mixing bowl, whisk the plain flour, tapioca flour, baking powder and salt together with 250 ml (9 fl oz/1 cup) water to form a smooth, thin batter.

Heat a cast-iron frying pan over a high heat. Add 2 tablespoons of vegetable oil to the pan and coat the base well, then add half the oyster meat and stir-fry for 1 minute, or until the oyster juices have evaporated. Pour half of the batter over the oysters, then quickly swirl the pan in a circular motion to coat the base evenly.

Crack an egg over the mixture and, using a rubber spatula, scrape everything toward the centre of the pan to form a circular omelette around 15 cm (6 in) in diameter. Cook for 2 minutes, loosening around the edges, until golden brown on the bottom.

Cut the omelette into four pieces and turn each piece to cook and brown the other side. Transfer the omelette to a serving platter and cover to keep warm, then repeat this process with the remaining ingredients to make a second omelette.

Once you have completed your second omelette, prepare the topping. Return the pan to the stove, add the vegetable oil and heat until smoking. Add the garlic, bean sprouts and spring onion and stir-fry for 30 seconds, then add the fish sauce and white pepper and stir-fry for another 30 seconds.

To serve, spoon the topping over the oyster omelettes, drizzle over the sriracha chilli sauce and garnish with the coriander.

RED PORK WITH RICE, CRACKLING & ORANGE EGG

KHAO MOO DAENG	Si Morakot, 80–82 Soi Sukon 1, between Hua Lamphong Station and Chinatown	THB 50.00 AUD $2.00

Si Morakot has been in operation for over 60 years and in these premises since 1977; originally it was a street stall that became extraordinarily successful so the owners set up in a shop-house. You find it at 80–82 Soi Sukon 1, between Hua Lamphong station and Chinatown, where it's open from 11 am–2 pm for lunch then from 7 pm onwards for dinner. The place is always packed and you invariably have to line up – a 30 minute wait is fairly standard – but it's worth it for the roast pork and barbecue pork, all cooked over charcoal, that they specialise in. Family-run, the owners are much loved in these parts and they seem to know all their customers. And wow, the meat they cook; it's so delicious and you can tell how much care they take with everything. The crackling is always spot-on, the meat is always juicy and their sauce (made from peanuts, sesame oil, tapioca flour, palm sugar and fermented soybeans) is consistently perfect. You order a plate of their pork and it comes, sliced, with rice, crackling, pieces of Chinese sausage, lots of chopped bird's eye chilli, spring onions, cucumber, a soft-boiled egg (stained orange!) and that lovely thick sauce. If you are lucky enough to score an inside table you'll be offered a clear soup too and make sure you say yes to that. Made using pork bones, it's brimming with meaty, savoury, slow-cooked goodness. And if, by some chance, you find yourself wanting something more to eat, you can also pick up great satay from Chong Kee right next door.

GREEN PAPAYA SALAD WITH SALTED FIELD CRAB

SOM TUM PLA RA

**SERVES 4–6
AS PART OF A SHARED MEAL**

1 garlic clove, sliced
1 tablespoon unsalted roasted peanuts
4 bird's eye chillies
4 snake (yard-long) beans,
   cut into 3 cm (1¼ in) lengths
2 salted rice field crabs (see glossary)
1 tablespoon shaved palm
   sugar (jaggery)
5 cherry tomatoes, cut in half
1 teaspoon acacia seeds (see glossary)
200 g (7 oz) green papaya, shredded
2 tablespoons Tamarind Water
   (see page 152)
½ tablespoon mam nem (fermented
   anchovy sauce; see glossary)
juice of ½ lime
1 tablespoon fish sauce
lime wedges, to serve

Here's a classic northern Thai salad that is fairly well known. But what you may not know is that there are different versions, not just one. One of the most unusual – and also my favourite – is this one, though it packs a flavour punch which might be an acquired taste for some. You should definitely try it, however. In Thailand when you order som tum from a street or market stall, all the ingredients are muddled fresh right in front of you, in a traditional clay mortar using a wooden pestle. They're gently bruised, rather than pounded, and the sound this makes is distinctive and rather like drumming. The process is interactive too – the idea is, you tell them how many chillies you want (two? five? ten?) and then taste as they mix your som tum, letting them know if you want it more sour, spicy or fish-saucy. They'll adjust the flavour balance to your individual preference and you should feel free to do that with this recipe as well. Here, you've got the standard green papaya, snake beans and cherry tomatoes but also some salted crab and acacia seeds together with a pungent dressing based on fermented anchovy sauce (which is a bit like shrimp paste, only stronger). The crabs are small crabs from rice paddy fields and they're fermented whole in salted water. In Thailand, cooks use the salty preserving brine as a seasoning sauce in their cooking, so nothing gets wasted.

Using a large mortar and pestle, pound the garlic to a paste. Add the peanuts and chillies and pound until mixed with the garlic.

Now add the snake beans and salted crab, gently pounding while adding the palm sugar, tomatoes, acacia seeds and papaya. Continue gently pounding and mixing with a spoon at the same time.

Next add the tamarind water, mam nem, lime juice and fish sauce. Lightly pound and mix for a further minute, for all the flavours to infuse.

Transfer to a bowl and serve straight away with the lime wedges.

GLASS NOODLES WOK-TOSSED WITH SEAFOOD, WATER MIMOSA & CHILLI

MEE PAD PAK TALAY	Saw Nah Wang, 156/2 Dinso Road, Sao Chingcha	THB 65.00 AUD $2.50

At 156/2 Dinso Road there's a restaurant run by an all-woman crew. Called Saw Nah Wang, it's a typical old shop-house restaurant, with vintage family portraits on the walls and very simple decor. Open from 10 am–11 pm, it's tiny, gets very crammed at lunchtime and serves truly tasty food. They're famous for their noodle dishes, which the chef-owner has been turning out for around 35 years – no-one else is allowed near the wok to cook them, only her. The dish that put her on the map is this one, glass noodles with seafood and water mimosa. It's cooked over extremely high heat, with glass noodles, prawns (shrimp), squid, water mimosa, tons of garlic and chilli all tossed together in a hot wok for about 2 minutes. The chilli pervades the restaurant and it's so intense that you'll almost end up coughing. To serve, fresh chilli goes on top, then a squeeze of lime and that's it. The water mimosa is a unique aquatic vegetable that's popular in Thailand and Vietnam and one you can easily buy from Asian greengrocers. It has beautiful feathered leaves; I love looking at it, but of course, it's also really great to eat – either raw, or wok-tossed, as here.

**Slow-Braised
Pork Hock
in Soy &
Coconut Juice**
Khao Kha Moo

< 288

SERVES 4-6
AS PART OF A SHARED MEAL

SLOW-BRAISED PORK HOCK IN SOY & COCONUT JUICE

KHAO KHA MOO

2 x 1 kg (2 lb 4 oz) pork hocks
vegetable oil, for deep-frying
4 coriander (cilantro) roots,
    scraped clean and chopped
4 garlic cloves, crushed
10 white peppercorns, crushed
6 cm (2½ in) piece of fresh ginger,
    sliced
2 black cardamom pods
    (see glossary), bruised
3 star anise
5 cm (2 in) piece of cassia bark
1 tablespoon liquid palm sugar
    (see glossary) or shaved dark
    palm sugar (jaggery)
4 tablespoons light soy sauce
2 tablespoons dark soy sauce
500 ml (18 fl oz/2 cups) Chicken
    Stock (see page 214)
1 litre (35 fl oz/4 cups) young coconut
    juice (see glossary)
2 hard-boiled eggs, peeled and halved
1 handful coriander (cilantro) leaves,
    to garnish

TO SERVE
200 g (7 oz) gai lan (Chinese broccoli),
    sliced into 3 cm (1¼ in) lengths
    and blanched
steamed jasmine rice
Soy & Chilli Dipping Sauce
    (see page 164)

No visit I've ever made to Bangkok has been complete without a trip to Sukhumvit Soi 38. This is one of the oldest and most iconic street food destinations in Bangkok but unhappily it's disappearing – when I stopped by recently, I was upset to see that many of the vendors had already moved to make way for a new development. By February 2017 the whole block will be gone and that will be the end of a street-eating era. Thankfully though, my favourite vendor from here has only moved to Soi 42, not so far away. He cooks pork hock, slow braised in soy, coconut juice, cassia, star anise and other aromatics. I love this dish! The hock cooks until it falls off the bone, by which time the skin is silky soft and gelatinous and the meat, fall-apart tender. There's so much flavour swimming about in the cooking liquor you just need some steamed gai lan and rice to go with the pork and you've got a terrific meal.

Place the hocks in a saucepan with enough cold salted water to cover. Bring to the boil and cook for 3 minutes, skimming off any impurities. Drain, wash under cold water, then drain again and pat dry.

Half-fill a wok or large saucepan with vegetable oil and heat to 180°C (350°F), or until a cube of bread dropped into the oil browns in 15 seconds. Add the hocks and cook for 3 minutes on each side, or until lightly browned. The oil can spit violently, so cover the wok with a splatter guard if the oil spits too much. Remove the hocks and drain.

Heat 1 tablespoon of the deep-frying oil in a saucepan. Stir-fry the coriander roots, garlic, peppercorns and ginger over a medium–high heat until fragrant. Add the cardamom, star anise and cassia and fry for a further minute.

Add the sugar, soy sauces, stock and coconut juice. Bring to the boil. Add the hocks, and a little water if needed to cover them. Bring back to the boil and skim off any impurities. Reduce the heat, cover slightly with a lid, then simmer for 3½–4 hours, or until the meat begins to fall off the bone.

Take the pan off the heat. Transfer the hocks to a shallow serving bowl, add the halved eggs, then pour over the cooking liquor. Garnish with coriander and serve with gai lan, steamed jasmine rice, and a soy and chilli dipping sauce.

WON TON SOUP WITH EGG NOODLES & CRABMEAT

BA MEE

250 g (9 oz) minced (ground) pork
½ teaspoon sugar
½ teaspoon Garlic Oil (see page 214)
½ teaspoon sesame oil
pinch of salt
¼ teaspoon white pepper
¼ egg white
16 sheets of 7 cm (2¾ in) square
    fresh won ton wrappers
1 litre (35 fl oz/4 cups) Pork & Chicken
    Stock (see page 292)
400 g (14 oz) fresh thin egg noodles
100 g (3½ oz) cooked crabmeat
½ bunch watercress
½ bunch coriander (cilantro) leaves
6 spring onions (scallions), sliced
½ bunch garlic chives, sliced into
    4 cm (1½ in) lengths
1 lemon, quartered
100 g (3½ oz) bean sprouts
2 red bird's eye chillies, sliced
fish sauce, to serve

My favourite ever won ton soup vendor has been at Sukhumvit Soi 38 for 40 years and I'm hoping he stays here, even after the whole block has been demolished. His stall is slightly separate from the part of this strip that's being torn down, so I'm hopeful. He's so friendly and humble and what I love about this dish is the way he makes everything himself from scratch. The noodles, the stock and the won tons, they're all made so expertly by him. When you order a bowl, it comes with slices of his barbecued pork plus a garnish of fresh crabmeat; you don't often get such special touches when you have this dish. Won ton noodle soup is considered comfort food and the kind of thing people eat when they're maybe not feeling so well. But I like it any time, and I enjoy making it. It's easy – you don't need to make your own noodles the way my man does, but you should certainly make your own stock.

Put the pork, sugar, garlic oil, sesame oil, salt, pepper and egg white in a bowl and mix well to combine. Lay the won ton wrappers out on a bench with one corner of each wrapper facing you. Place a teaspoon of the pork filling in the centre of the won ton, brush the top two edges with water and fold the bottom up to create a triangle; push down on the edges to seal them. Brush the two bottom corners with water, bring them together and press to seal. Fold the remaining corner backwards and press to secure against the back of the won ton. Repeat this process, placing each completed won ton under a damp cloth to keep them moist. Bring a large saucepan of water to the boil. Add the won tons and cook for 2 minutes, then remove and refresh them in iced water. Place the won tons in a colander and set aside.

To serve the won ton noodles, put the pork stock in a saucepan and bring to the boil. Meanwhile, divide the egg noodles into four portions and blanch them separately for 20 seconds, then refresh in iced water. This allows the noodles to develop a nice firmness. Return them to the boiling water for 10 seconds, then place them in the serving bowls.

Now place the won tons back in the boiling water to heat through, then transfer to the bowls.

Pour the boiling broth over the noodles, top with 1 tablespoon of crabmeat into each bowl, and garnish with the watercress, coriander, spring onions and garlic chives.

Serve with lemon wedges and bean sprouts on the side, along with sliced chilli and fish sauce to dip.

**Won Ton
Soup with Egg
Noodles &
Crabmeat**
Ba Mee Kreaw

289 >

TOASTED RICE POWDER

MAKES 100 G (3½ OZ)

100 g (3½ oz/½ cup) sticky (glutinous) rice

This is an essential ingredient in many northern Thai salads like laab and red ant egg salad (see page 227). The toasted rice is slightly gritty, giving an added textural dimension as well as a nutty flavour to dishes – it also acts to slightly thicken juices and dressings. Always use white sticky (glutinous) rice when making this and don't be tempted by the store-bought equivalent; it tastes nothing like freshly made toasted rice powder.

Heat a frying pan or wok over a medium heat and dry-roast the rice for 8–10 minutes, until lightly browned, tossing occasionally. (For a smokier flavour, allow the rice to turn a deeper shade of brown; to make your rice powder more perfumed, you can also dry-roast the rice with chilli, lemongrass and makrut (kaffir lime) leaves.)

Remove from the heat and allow to cool, then pound to a powder using a large mortar and pestle. It is best used fresh, but can be stored in an airtight container in a cool, dark place for several weeks.

PORK & CHICKEN STOCK

MAKES 6 LITRES (210 FL OZ/24 CUPS)

2 x 1.6 kg (3 lb 8 oz) whole chickens, quartered
8 pork hip bones
140 g (5 oz) salt
1 dried flounder
2 dried squid
125 ml (4 fl oz/½ cup) fish sauce
220 g (8 oz) sugar

Once you've cooked this fantastic stock, you'll come to appreciate all that goes into the making of deceptively simple dishes like won ton noodles or pan mee (see pages 203 and 190). Not that it is in any way difficult; quite the opposite. Dried squid and dried flounder are common ingredients that you'll find in Chinese grocers. They don't so much give a fishy flavour as round everything out with an amazing savouriness that's hard to describe. They also give the stock extra body. Pork hip bones are preferred here as they are a particularly good source of marrow, which adds even more flavour and body.

Soak the chickens and pork bones in cold water with 2 tablespoons of the salt for 2 hours. Discard the water, then wash the chickens and bones under cold water and set aside. Chargrill the dried fish and squid over a low heat until browned. Remove and scrape off any burnt bits with a knife. Wrap the fish and squid up in muslin (cheesecloth).

Add the chickens and pork bones to a large saucepan and cover with 10 litres (350 fl oz/40 cups) cold water. Place over a high heat and bring to the boil, skimming constantly. Once boiled, reduce the heat, continue to cook and occasionally skim for 1 hour. Add the muslin bag and reduce the heat further, until the water is barely rolling over. Cover with a lid and cook for 4 hours.

Once cooked, pass the stock through a double muslin sieve into another saucepan. Add the fish sauce, remaining salt and sugar, and return to a simmer, skim off any impurities, then allow to cool. Transfer the stock to smaller containers and store in the refrigerator for up to 3 days, or freeze until required.

PRAWN HEAD STOCK

MAKES 2 LITRES (70 FL OZ/8 CUPS)

1 kg (2 lb 4 oz) large raw prawn (shrimp) heads
1 large leek, trimmed and cut into large chunks
2 garlic cloves
2 cm (¾ in) piece of fresh ginger, sliced
1 makrut (kaffir lime) leaf
½ bunch coriander (cilantro), stems and roots only

In any food culture worth its salt, very little is wasted and nowhere is this truer than throughout Asia. Prawn heads make the best kind of stock, which in turn makes all the difference to a good, home-made tom yum soup (see page 246). So whenever you buy raw prawns, instead of throwing out the heads, freeze them until you collect enough to make this stock.

Place the prawn heads in a large saucepan with 2 litres (70 fl oz/8 cups) of water and bring to the boil. Skim off any impurities, then add the rest of the ingredients. Return to the boil, then reduce the heat and simmer for 30 minutes. Strain through a fine sieve and allow to cool. Store in the fridge for up to 3 days, or freeze until required.

GLOSSARY

ACACIA SEEDS

Acacia has a long history of use by Indigenous Australian people. It is also widely eaten throughout South-East Asia. The seeds are extremely nutritious and contain several times the protein of wheat. The seeds can be eaten raw, roasted or steamed and eaten as a snack or added to salads.

ASIAN CELERY

Much smaller than regular celery, the leaves resemble parsley, and the thin stalks, which have a delicate yet fragrant flavour, are stringless and crisp.

BETEL LEAVES

The glossy, heart-shaped leaves of a perennial creeping plant. Betel leaves are chewed raw for their mild stimulant properties, and used widely throughout South-East Asia in both raw and cooked dishes, most often as a wrapper for salad and other ingredients.

BLACK CARDAMOM

A large, black-brown pod with a camphor-like aroma, used whole as a spice. Its fragrance is also somewhat smoky, as traditionally it is dried over an open fire. The more common green cardamom pods cannot be substituted.

BLACK FUNGUS (WOOD EAR)

Most commonly available dried, this Chinese mushroom is also called wood ear and tree ear mushroom, as it is said to resemble ears on the trees it grows out of. The dried mushrooms need to be soaked for about 20 minutes before using, and have a firm texture with a deep, earthy flavour.

CANDLENUTS

A relative of macadamia nuts that resembles them in appearance and in texture, candlenuts are used in Malaysian and Indonesian cuisine as a thickener and a texture enhancer in curries and other dishes. Eaten cooked only (as raw they are slightly toxic and taste bitter), they are often pounded or ground into pastes before being added to curries, sambals or stews.

STAR FRUIT (CARAMBOLA)

Popular throughout South-East Asia, the star fruit is a longish tropical fruit with distinct ridges running down its sides. When cut widthways the cross-section resembles a star (hence the name 'star fruit'). The entire fruit is edible and is usually eaten raw, although it can also be made into relishes, preserves and juices.

DRIED SHRIMP

Widely used throughout South-East Asia, dried shrimp is favoured for the special 'umami' or 'fifth taste' it brings to dishes. Dried shrimp is often soaked and/or pounded before using. It is easy to find in any Asian supermarket. Fresh prawns (shrimp) cannot be substituted.

INDONESIAN PRAWN CRACKERS (KERUPUK)

Made predominantly from starch with prawn used for flavouring, these crackers are a popular snack across South-East Asia but are most closely associated with Indonesia and Malaysia. In Indonesia, the term 'krupuk' or 'kerupuk' refers to the type of relatively large crackers, while 'kripik' or 'keripik' refers to smaller bite-size crackers. The crackers are deep-fried and puff up before being eaten as a snack or cracked and sprinkled on top of dishes such as gado gado to add crispy texture.

KECAP MANIS

An Indonesian sweetened aromatic soy sauce, which has a dark colour, a thick, syrupy consistency and a unique, pronounced, sweet and somewhat molasses-like flavour. It is used in marinades, as a condiment or as an ingredient in Indonesian cooking. The sweetness comes from palm sugar; other flavourings include garlic and star anise.

LAP CHEONG

A cured, dried raw-meat sausage which is quite hard in texture, and requires cooking before eating. Lap cheong is the Cantonese name for wind-dried Chinese sausage, and literally means 'wax sausage', referring to the waxy look and texture of the sausage. It is readily available from Asian supermarkets, where it is sold in vacuum packets.

LIQUID PALM SUGAR

This is fresh sap, harvested from sago or sugar palms, and boiled. Most commonly palm sugar is available in dried form, as it is more convenient to transport. However, the fresh sap has a smooth, syrupy texture, is easier to use and has a more subtle flavour.

MAM NEM

A sauce made from fermented salted anchovies, widely used as a condiment in Vietnamese cooking. It has a more pungent aroma and flavour than regular fish sauce. It is sold in bottles in Asian food stores.

GLOSSARY

MAM RUOC

A pungent Vietnamese fermented shrimp paste, made from mashed marinated shrimps. The paste has an intense smell and flavour and is packed in bottles. You'll find it in Asian supermarkets.

MUSTARD GREENS

Part of the brassica family, mustard greens belong to the same genus as the plants that produce mustard seeds, and have a similarly strong flavour. They are often preserved as a salty pickle, which is readily available from Asian supermarkets.

PANDAN LEAVES

Pandan is a herbaceous tropical plant that grows in South-East Asia, known in Chinese as 'fragrant plant' because of its unique, sweet aroma. The bright green leaves are used in Thai and South-East Asian cuisines to lend a unique taste and aroma to both sweet and savoury dishes and are available fresh or frozen in Asian grocers.

PERILLA LEAVES

Also called shiso, this highly fragranced herb is a member of the mint family. Its large, delicate, rounded leaves have a jagged edge, and can be green or purple. Perilla is used in salads and in a number of stews and simmered dishes.

ROCK SUGAR

Rock sugar is a crystalised, unrefined sugar that can be white or golden. It retains the sugar cane's delicate, smoky flavour and is used as a base for phở and other Vietnamese soup dishes.

SALTED RICE FIELD CRABS

Salted rice field crabs are small crabs from rice paddy fields, which have been fermented whole in salt water. In Thailand, cooks use the salty preserving brine as a seasoning in their cooking, so nothing is wasted. The rice field crab adds a great flavour and distinctive aroma when pounded up in Thai tom sum salad.

SAMBAL OELEK

A staple of Indonesian and Malaysian cooking, sambal oelek is a hot sauce made in its purest form simply from ground chillies with a little salt and vinegar – though a variety of other ingredients including shrimp paste, fish sauce, garlic, palm sugar, ginger, lime juice and rice vinegar are often also added. It is widely available in Asian grocery stores and supermarkets.

SAW-TOOTH CORIANDER (CILANTRO)

Native to South America and related to regular coriander, this herb has a relatively large, oblong, bright green leaf with serrated sides. It has a much stronger flavour than regular coriander and is used in a variety of dishes – both raw in salads, and cooked in stir-fries, noodle dishes, soups and curries.

SHAOXING RICE WINE

A famous sweetish Chinese cooking wine from the town of the same name in eastern China, near Shanghai. It is brewed from rice and is readily available from Asian supermarkets.

SOM MOO FERMENTED PORK SAUSAGE

A traditional celebratory food in Vietnam, som moo is made from fermented raw minced (ground) pork and shredded pork skin. It is available from Vietnamese grocers and many Asian supermarkets in small packets or large blocks and can be either eaten as sold or cooked.

THAI ROASTED RED CHILLI PASTE

A staple of Thai cooking, this spicy, sweet condiment is used in a variety of dishes ranging from soups and salads to stir-fries. Made from a mix of fresh and dried chillies together with a varying combination of other ingredients often including roasted shrimp paste, tamarind pulp, palm sugar, fish sauce, shallots and garlic, it is widely available in jars from Asian grocers and supermarkets.

YOUNG COCONUT JUICE

The clear, watery liquid that develops inside immature coconuts. It is a popular drink and a commonly used liquid in cooking.

Luke Nguyen is one of Australia's best loved chefs. He is the owner of Sydney and Brisbane's acclaimed Red Lantern and Fat Noodle restaurants, and is a regular presenter on SBS where his television shows have taken him all over the world. His recent series, *Luke Nguyen's Street Food Asia*, is the companion TV show to this book.

Luke is also the author of six previous cookbooks: *Secrets of the Red Lantern, Indochine, The Songs of Sapa, China to Vietnam, France* and *The Food of Vietnam, the ultimate companion to authentic Vietnamese cooking.* Luke currently splits his time between Australia and Vietnam, where he has recently opened his own cooking school – Grain – in Saigon.

redlantern.com.au

DEDICATION

I dedicate this book to my twin boys, Kian and Kohl, who entered this crazy world just as I began writing this book.

I so much look forward to the day when you can both travel and share all these wonderful street food experiences with me.

ACKNOWLEDGEMENTS

I am very grateful to have such a passionate and talented team behind this book.

Thank you to Jane Willson and the entire Hardie Grant crew for believing in me and putting this all together.

Andrea O'Connor, thank you for your guidance, but most of all your patience.

Simon Davis, thank you for making my recipes and words make sense.

Evi O, thank you for introducing me to your awesome quirky, artistic design world.

And to my family, Alan Benson, Leanne Kitchen and Lynne Nguyen. This book would not have been possible without your incredible talent, tireless work and great support.

INDEX

INDEX

INDEX

INDEX

Published in 2016 by Hardie Grant Books, an imprint of
Hardie Grant Publishing

Hardie Grant Books (Melbourne)
Ground Floor, Building 1
658 Church Street
Richmond, Victoria 3121
www.hardiegrant.com.au

Hardie Grant Books (London)
5th & 6th Floors
52–54 Southwark Street
London SE1 1UN
www.hardiegrant.co.uk

A Cataloguing-in-Publication entry is
available from the catalogue of the
National Library of
Australia at www.nla.gov.au.
Street Food Asia
ISBN 978 1 74379 219 3

Publishing Director: Jane Willson
Project Editor: Andrea O'Connor
Editor: Simon Davis
Designer: Evi O / OetomoNew
Photographer: Alan Benson
Production Manager: Todd Rechner

Colour reproduction by
Splitting Image Colour Studio.
Printed in China by
1010 Printing International Limited.